Subject Leader Guide for English

Contents

Subject leader information

National Curriculum for Key Stages 1–3

Book End, Range Road, Witney, Oxfordshire, OX29 0YD

www.scholastic.co.uk

© 2014, Scholastic Ltd

1 2 3 4 5 6 7 8 9   4 5 6 7 8 9 0 1 2 3

British Library Cataloguing-in-Publication Data
A catalogue record for this book is available from the
British Library.

ISBN 978-1407-14063-6

Authors
Rebecca Cosgrave, Primary Literacy Adviser
Richard Durrant, Secondary English Adviser

Editorial
Melissa Somers, Jennie Clifford and Rachel Morgan

Design
Tracey Camden

Cover design
Nicolle Thomas

References

Myhill D, Jones S, Watson A, Lines H *Playful
Explicitness with Grammar: a pedagogy for writing
from Literacy Volume 47 no. 2* (UKLA July 2013)

Ofsted *Moving English Forwards* (2012)

UKLA Writing Fact Cards (2014) www.ukla.org

Useful websites

Talk for Writing: www.talk4writing.co.uk

National Literacy Trust: www.literacytrust.org.uk

Literacy Shed: www.literacyshed.com

Babcock LDP www.babcock-education.co.uk/ldp/

Babcock LDP is part of the UK's leading education
support and improvement service with a proven
track record of working in partnership with education
establishments to improve outcomes for children and
young people.

MIX
Paper from
responsible sources
FSC® C011748

Introduction

The new National Curriculum for 2014 places particular pressures on subject leaders in primary and secondary schools in maintaining high quality teaching, effective use of resources and improved standards at a time of curriculum change.

Scholastic Education, publisher of the bestselling *100 Lessons* series, has partnered with Babcock Learning and Development Partnership, one of the UK's leading school improvement services, to develop these essential subject guides, which can be used to support your colleagues in understanding and responding to the curriculum changes.

For the first time, the Department for Education has made the new National Curriculum for 2014 available in digital format only. We understand that a printed copy of the Curriculum is a useful tool in communicating these changes and as such a complete printed programme of study for English Key Stages 1–3 has been included in each Subject Leader's Guide.

Each guide also offers:

- Explanation of the changes to the curriculum in England and the subject leader's role in implementing these changes
- Information on Ofsted's expectations and role in inspecting English teaching in your school.
- Advice on the priority areas for Key Stages 1–2
- Support for structuring the curriculum including advice on lesson planning and creativity in the new curriculum.
- A checklist for managing the move towards the new National Curriculum is also supplied.

We hope this Subject Leader's Guide proves to be a useful tool and wish you every success in implementing the new curriculum in your school.

Scholastic Education   Babcock LDP

Overview of main changes to the English curriculum KS1-2

Phonics

The content of phonics has changed little from current best practice: rigorous, systematic phonics is now a statutory requirement. Schools using phonics programmes that meet the current criteria (see page 17) will find little change in either content or expectations. There are some changes in detail and emphasis such as: verb endings (suffixes) have been moved from Year 2 into Year 1; Year 2 phonics is focused more on spelling with an expectation that phonics for decoding is secured by the end of Year 1; pupils who are not secure in these skills by the end of KS1 will need to continue the phonics teaching to catch up with their peers.

Focus on essential skills

Grammar: Teachers will be familiar with much of the content already, although the expectations of pupils' mastering of terminology are new. The curriculum details clearly when aspects of grammar should be introduced. There is an expectation that once introduced, grammatical understanding is developed through revision in subsequent years.

Spelling: Again, the majority of the content is not new to teachers, but the level of detail has been amended. Statutory word lists have been introduced and give a clear indication of expected spelling levels. Teachers will need to address the content of the spelling curriculum and ensure that there is a clear and consistent approach to spelling strategies.

Reading for pleasure

The curriculum states that *schools should do everything to promote wider reading*. There is an expectation that this includes effective library provision and ambitious expectations for reading at home. Within the Programme of Study, reading is separated into: word reading and comprehension. The comprehension strand includes frequent reference to reading for pleasure.

Spoken language

Spoken language is described as having two strands: using discussion in order to learn, and being competent in the arts of speaking and listening (formal presentations, demonstrating to others and taking part in debate). Speaking and listening expectations can be found in the separate spoken language Programme of Study, but also within the Programmes of Study for reading and writing.

Coverage to process

One of the most significant changes is that the new curriculum does not specify genres to be covered, but broadly talks about a range of text types. Therefore, in many schools, the way English is planned across the medium and longer term will need to adapt. There is a new emphasis on developing the process of writing, which includes: establishing positive attitudes; developing stamina; planning/drafting; proofreading and editing. The contexts for developing these skills and processes are for schools to determine.

The subject leader's role KS1-3

What will Ofsted inspectors expect to see?

Judgements about the curriculum will be made as part of the wider review of the quality of leadership and management. Inspectors will consider how well leaders and managers ensure that the curriculum:

- focuses on the necessary priorities to ensure that all pupils make excellent progress in reading, writing and mathematics
- is broad and balanced (in the context of the school) and meets the needs, aptitudes and interest of pupils including pupils in the sixth form
- promotes high levels of achievement and good behaviour
- promotes the spiritual, moral, social and cultural development of all pupils, including the extent to which schools engage their pupils in extra-curricular activity and volunteering within their local community
- is effectively planned and taught
- does not compromise pupils' achievement, success or progression by inappropriately early entry to public examinations.

English subject leader's role

The main role of the subject leader is to manage the change to the new English curriculum, within the context of the changes to the whole curriculum, while maintaining and improving standards. In many ways, the school needs to have a clear direction about how the wider curriculum will be managed, before fundamental changes to English are made.

In supporting subject leaders with identifying the changes to English provision and practice, different schools will need to address different aspects. The order below is a suggested pathway, but it will depend on each school's priorities. Use it to focus review and development of the provision and practice of the English curriculum by clearly identifying current achievements as well as areas for improvement.

- Evaluate attainment and progress:
  - How well are pupils doing in relation to national standards?
  - Are pupils making good or better progress?
  - Are there differences in attainment or progress across the school?
    - Groups of pupils, such as FSM/boys/girls?
    - Key stages, cohorts or classes?
- Identify pedagogical approaches which are effective:
  - How do we teach this area currently?
  - Is the teaching approach consistent across the school?
  - Are there areas of significant expertise or weakness?
  - How do staff feel about teaching in this area?
  - How do pupils feel about their learning in this area?
- Identify staff subject knowledge strengths and areas for development:
  - Does everyone feel confident to deliver the expectations of the new curriculum?
  - What evidence is there that staff are confident about their subject knowledge?

- Consider the needs of your school community:
  - How well does the English curriculum reflect your location and the needs of the pupils?
  - Are pupils' interests met through the English curriculum?

While English subject leaders will need to fit with the whole-school development plan for the new curriculum, there are ways of approaching the specific challenges of English that could follow a suggested order:

1. Audit grammar and spelling subject knowledge, attainment and pedagogy.

2. Create an action plan to ensure that the statutory expectations in these areas will be met.

3. Audit current approaches to teaching reading, including use of the library, home reading and reading to pupils.

4. Review the approach to English teaching, with an emphasis on writing.
   - Consider the process of writing: planning/drafting/editing/proofreading.
   - Consider the contexts for English teaching – on what do we base blocks of work? How do we link English to the wider curriculum? How do we approach grammar teaching within English blocks?

What to do with this information?

Subject leaders might find it useful to consider drawing up a short-, medium- and long-term plan to address the issues arising from the review.

Short-term plans: What do I need to do now?

- The aim of a short-term plan is to manage immediate change.
- These might be termly action plans with clearly measurable criteria and detailed actions and monitoring.
- Actions plans should be evaluated regularly.

Medium-term plans: What do I want to achieve over a school year?

- This might take the form of a flexible termly overview plan, outlining the priorities for each short-term plan to ensure actions are achieved.
- It would be useful to set evaluation criteria for the medium-term plan in order to measure a rate of success.

Long-term plans: What needs to be done eventually?

- It is helpful to make a record of all the developments that need to be put in place over a much longer timescale.
- This should be based on the school's vision, and perhaps on a vision for English within the school.
- It is from the long-term plan that future medium-term priorities can be drawn to ensure that, as well as meeting new expectations, the school remains focused on its own priorities and vision for raising standards.

Priority areas in English KS1–2

For some time, teachers have been planning and teaching across blocks of work in English, leading towards a key written outcome. Under the new curriculum, the content of these blocks is no longer specified, but the approach remains fundamental. Within the statutory requirements, reference is made to pupils using models of text to support their own writing, as well as learning texts and developing the process of writing over time. When considering how to plan for the implementation of the new National Curriculum, subject leaders need to use this as a basis.

A key element of an effective implementation of the curriculum would therefore seem to be to continue to develop and improve teaching sequences for English. There are various models of planning teaching sequences, but the key elements are:

- using high-quality, authentic text models
- an engaging, purposeful writing outcome
- Assessment for Learning used to inform planning
- teaching grammar and punctuation in context
- Talk for Writing strategies used to enhance the quality of pupils' writing throughout the sequence
- phonics and spelling planned discretely, running alongside teaching sequences.

One model of teaching sequences, which subject leaders may find useful, can be found on page 19. This model has been developed by Babcock LDP and is based closely on Pie Corbett's Talk for Writing approaches. In this model, pupils move through *Imitate*, *Innovate* and *Invent*, enabling them to learn and remember texts, practise writing closely based on a model and apply independently with their own choice of writing outcome.

Key elements of teaching sequences developed

Use of high-quality, authentic texts

If pupils are to write high-quality, interesting and engaging texts, they need to read and explore texts of the highest quality. Teachers should choose a single, core text as the basis for the teaching sequence rather than multiple examples. This enables teachers and pupils to explore texts in depth rather than focusing on surface features. The models used should:

- have layers of meaning and content worth talking about, engaging pupils with the issues or themes. This might involve linking to particular interests of pupils
- have a clear structure that can be used as a scaffold for independent writing
- demonstrate rich and varied language features, enabling pupils to explore sentence- and word-level features in context, identifying the impact on the reader.

An engaging and purposeful writing outcome

Key literature on teaching writing informs us that:

- when pupils learn to write they are 'learning to represent aspects of their world' and therefore, in order to shape their texts, they need to draw on their personal interpretations of the world and the events they experience in it;
- pupils are active participants in their own learning and that they attempt to make meaning from school-based writing practices.

(From *UKLA Writing Fact Cards,* 2014. Sources: Christie, 2003; Cremin and Myhill, 2012)

When planning for an effective written outcome to a teaching sequence, consider the following questions.

- What do the pupils need to have learned by the end of this sequence of lessons?
- How will they demonstrate their learning?
- Are there clear success criteria?
- What will need to be taught so that they can all be successful?
- What form will it take?
- Does there need to be differentiated outcomes?
- How long will it take?

Pupils' written outcomes need to reflect the model text in terms of structure and language features used, but allow for individual interpretation and choice about content and adaptations they would like to make as it should be as independent as possible.

Assessment for Learning used to inform planning

Assessment for Learning (AfL) should impact on planning in at least the following ways.

- Choice of text model, genre and language features taught within a sequence should relate to the pupils' interests and next steps. For this reason it is not easy or advisable to map out a whole year's worth of English teaching in advance.
- Once a sequence has been chosen and outlined, AfL should influence the emphasis placed on elements within it. For example, completing an elicitation task at the start of a sequence will enable a teacher to adjust success criteria and detail of teaching within the sequence to accurately meet the needs of the whole class.
- Outlining a teaching sequence over two to three weeks enables teachers to use day-to-day AfL information to adjust the pace and manner of working towards the outcome.
- Throughout English teaching, pupils need to be encouraged to develop a reflective approach to their learning and, especially, their writing, so that they *develop the inner voice of a critically reflective writer* (*UKLA Writing Fact Cards*, 2014). Teachers need to create an ethos in the classroom where the writing process can be developed through effective dialogic talk and where pupils are actively involved in assessing and developing their own writing. The Transforming Writing project evaluation report provides some exciting and innovative approaches to developing this ethos, which can be found on the Literacy Trust's website.

◾SCHOLASTIC

Teaching grammar and punctuation in context

While expectations for grammar and punctuation teaching may have been raised within the new National Curriculum, and the introduction of the grammar, punctuation and spelling test may have focused schools on technical and accuracy issues, the most effective pedagogy for teaching grammar should be research-based and linked to writing and communication in a broader fashion. The work of Debra Myhill of Exeter University offers clear principles for effective teaching of grammar and punctuation.

- Grammatical metalanguage is used, but is always explained through examples and patterns.
- Links are made between the feature introduced and how it might enhance writing.
- Discussion is used to encourage critical conversations about language and effects.
- Creative imitation based on model patterns enables pupils to play with language and then use it in their own writing.
- Authentic examples are supplied from authentic texts.
- Activities should support pupils in making choices and being designers of writing.
- Language play, experimentation, risk-taking and games should be actively encouraged.

(Playful Explicitness with Grammar: a pedagogy for writing, Myhill et al., *Literacy*, volume 47 number 2, July 2013)

If these principles are to be implemented effectively, teachers need to embed the teaching of grammar into teaching sequences based on high-quality, authentic texts.

A different way of looking at the principles underpinning effective grammar teaching could be through a model such as 'A Connective Model for Grammar', based on a similar model developed by Haylock and Cockburn in the context of mathematics (1989). This model emphasises the need to link grammatical terminology to a context through talk, with the addition of a symbol to support understanding. This model has been developed to support the use of *Sentence Toolkit for Teachers: Bringing Grammar and Punctuation Alive in the Classroom* (Babcock LDP Literacy, 2013), which offers a visual image of a tool linked to each core grammatical concept and can also be augmented by a physical action. Use of an approach like this could form the basis of a whole-school approach to the teaching of grammar and punctuation.

Punctuation is essential to establish meaning in written communication. Subject leaders need to particularly attend to the teaching of punctuation and ensure that it is taught alongside grammar and writing, rather than as an add-on.

Talk for Writing strategies used to enhance the quality of pupils' writing throughout the sequence

'Talk for Writing' is an umbrella term for a range of strategies and approaches to teaching that aim to help pupils to externalise what is essentially an internal process, enabling teacher and writer to explore choices, decisions and ideas before and during the composition process. The core strategies are as follows:

- Learning and remembering texts
- Book talk
- Writer talk
- Warming up the word
- Purposeful sentence-level activities
- Boxing up the text.

For maximum effect, these strategies need to be developed within the *Imitate/Innovate/Invent* model for planning over a sequence of work:

Talk for Writing enables pupils to imitate the key language they need for a particular topic orally before they try reading and analysing it. Through fun activities that help them rehearse the tune of the language they need, followed by shared writing to show them how to craft their writing, pupils are helped to write in the same style.

(Talk for Writing website home page)

This approach is exemplified in the example sequence on page 19, and there is further information, support and resources on the Talk for Writing website.

Discrete planning of phonics and spelling

Subject leaders need to ensure that there is dedicated time for the teaching of phonics at KS1 and spelling at KS2. The majority of schools have daily, discrete sessions at KS1 for teaching the core knowledge and skills of phonics; this will need to continue, following a systematic phonics programme that matches the expectations of the new National Curriculum.

In addition, subject leaders need to ensure that teachers at KS2 also plan for regular teaching time for spelling. It is both useful and supportive to develop a sequence for teaching spelling that runs parallel to the main teaching sequence. This might be across two- or three-week blocks, focusing on a small cluster of linked objectives, using the following system.

- Revisit and review
- Teach
- Practice
- Apply
- Assess

There is a sample of this approach within an example termly programme for covering spelling objectives included on page 21.

Creativity and the new curriculum KS1–2

The aims for the National Curriculum clearly state:

The National Curriculum is just one element in the education of every child. There is time and the space in the school day and in each week, term and year to range beyond the National Curriculum specifications. The National Curriculum provides an outline of core knowledge around which teachers can develop exciting and stimulating lessons to promote the development of pupils' knowledge, understanding and skills as part of the wider school curriculum.

As a result, there is an expectation that every school and every teacher will build on the core to create an appropriate curriculum and lessons that are exciting and creative.

In terms of creativity within English, there are three key aspects to consider.

1. Linking English to the wider curriculum

There are many ways in which English can be locked into learning across the whole curriculum. This is particularly important to consider as subject leaders working with the whole school to build a new curriculum. Most teachers will already be using these ways to make English relevant and purposeful. To support subject leaders with considering the effectiveness of this, here is a summary of five of the most useful ways of building meaningful links.

- **Teaching concurrently:** this is where an aspect of English is taught at the same time as a linked area of learning across the curriculum. For example, we might teach how to write non-fiction reports in English using the content from our topic on the local area as the context for learning.

- **Directly teaching an aspect of English in another subject:** this may happen less frequently, but would be where a particular aspect of skill or knowledge from the English curriculum is taught through another subject, such as teaching the spelling of technical vocabulary (perhaps from the statutory word list) as part of a science lesson.

- **Using and applying English skills – planned and incidental:** this could include providing opportunities for pupils to use previous learning in another context. For example, a teacher may plan for the pupils to use explanatory writing skills, which were taught in a previous term, in the context of a technology project.

- **Using English teaching strategies in other curriculum areas:** an example of this could be the use of Talk for Writing strategies to support learning in other areas. For example, a teacher might use the strategy of learning and remembering texts to support pupils with remembering the sequence of the water cycle in science or use a vocabulary generation game to begin planning for a dance sequence.

- **Homework:** most teachers already link learning in this way – most homework is either written or reading based. This could be developed where learning is linked within the school day, or by using strategies from English to enhance home learning across the curriculum.

2. Using a wide variety of text forms to engage and inspire

Many teachers are already skilled at using visual and multimedia texts to enhance the English learning experience for pupils. The National Curriculum's lack of specificity about texts types to be covered enables teachers to develop this further. There are many places where visual texts can be accessed, including the Babcock LDP literacy website and The Literacy Shed, which offers a wide variety of really innovative ways of engaging with English through visual texts.

When using film to support writing there are a number of elements that can be considered, known as the 'Cs and Ss'. These are **c**haracter, **c**olour, **c**omposition, **c**utting (editing), **c**amera angle, **c**ategory and **s**ound, **s**etting, **s**tory, **s**equence and **s**ymbolism. Obviously, some of these relate to story in any medium but others relate only to film. If several of these are chosen, the film can be watched with the chosen elements as a particular focus. Once shared and discussed, words and phrases can be generated and then used in writing. For example, the time of day can be told through colour, as in *El Caminante* (story shorts from the BFI), which leads to showing writing rather than telling writing.

3. Offering a wide range of opportunities to create varied text forms as outcomes

In addition to using a wide variety of text types as models, pupils need opportunities to create texts in a variety of forms, which reflect the varied purposes and forms of communication in the world. The emphasis on the processes of writing with the National Curriculum can be developed in any written form of communication. Pupils need to experience blogging, comics, web design and multimedia texts as well as the more traditional forms. Linking English learning to pupils' experiences and the enormously exciting ways in which communication is enabled in the modern world can enable teachers to develop pupils' skills and knowledge in creative and stimulating contexts. Examples of this might be Book Creator, an iPad app or using Snap Guide, another application, to write instructions. For those with PCs, the Glogster website is an engaging way to create a multimedia text.

SCHOLASTIC

Managing the move towards the new National Curriculum KS1–3

First steps

- Become familiar with the National Curriculum.
- Focus initially on the statutory appendices for spelling and grammar.
  - Which of these is the greater priority in your school?
- For spelling, consider the following:
  - Is there enough time allocated to teach new expectations?
  - Can cohorts start at age-related expectations?
  - What support will staff need to implement this effectively?
- For grammar, consider the following:
  - How secure is subject knowledge?
  - Is grammar teaching embedded in a teaching sequence?
  - What are the grammar test results like?
- How developed is reading for pleasure?
  - Do all teachers read to pupils every day?
  - Do pupils in your school enjoy reading?
  - Are pupils reading enough in school time and at home, and how do you know?
  - Are library/book corners attractive and well used?
  - Are there any significant resourcing issues?
  - Is guided reading happening regularly across the school?

Following on from this

- What does the English curriculum look like in our school?
  - How do we decide what to teach?
  - What texts do we use?
  - How does the curriculum reflect the community?
  - Do teachers plan sequences over a period of weeks?
  - What strategies do we use to underpin our teaching of writing, for example, Talk for Writing?
  - How effectively are these embedded in practice and what impact do they have?
  - How do we approach the process of writing across the school (plan, draft, edit and proofread)? How consistent is this approach across the school?
- How do we make cross-curricular links and how effective are they?
  - Do pupils have opportunities to apply English skills across the rest of the curriculum?
  - Is writing across the curriculum of a similar standard to writing in English?
  - How will English link to changes to the rest of the curriculum?

Monitoring implementation of the new National Curriculum

Look at timetables showing where phonics, spelling and reading to pupils takes place.

- How much are pupils reading and what are they reading?
- Keep a cumulative record of text types (and text titles) covered for each class, each term.
- Review planning and pupils' books at least twice a year, focusing on one completed sequence of learning. Use a sample of pupils' work, including all books where they write. Look for:
  - coverage of grammar objectives through planning and key outcomes in writing
  - quality of teaching sequences
  - how Assessment for Learning informs teaching
  - pupils' spelling
  - planning, drafting, editing and proofreading
  - application of skills across the curriculum: opportunities and quality.

Evaluation

These key questions can be used to evaluate English overall or a specific area of development, such as phonics.

- Are pupils meeting age-related expectations and above as set out in the new National Curriculum?
- Are there any gaps or underachieving groups?
- Are pupils making at least expected progress. Are enough making better than expected progress?
- Is the quality of English teaching at least good or better?
- What further support and development is required?

SCHOLASTIC

Overview of changes to the Key Stage 3 curriculum KS3

It is highly unlikely that many English teachers will find the new KS3 curriculum objectionable, mainly because its slimness leaves little room for prescriptive detail. For example, the expectation that pupils will be taught to draw on their *knowledge of literary and rhetorical devices from their reading and listening to enhance the impact of their writing* is hardly going to outrage any practitioner. After all, the requirement does not come with a list of approved devices.

However, there are some interesting details, emphases and implications in the new, slim curriculum.

The approved authors who have haunted secondary English for so long have finally been laid to rest. Teachers are now given free choice of – for example – *high-quality works from…pre-1914*. Although pupils must read two plays by Shakespeare, no other author is named.

The status of literature has been reinforced in the opening section, the 'Purpose of study', which asserts that *through reading in particular, pupils have a chance to develop culturally, emotionally, intellectually, socially and spiritually. Literature, especially, plays a key role in such development.*

The curriculum has a renewed 'traditional' emphasis that no longer finds room for the multi-modal texts that are required study in the current curriculum. On the other hand, the new curriculum does insist on *a wide range of…non-fiction* as part of a pupils' reading diet.

The new curriculum's emphasis on ensuring pupils *develop the habit of reading widely and often, for both pleasure and information* is likely to be welcomed by all teachers, even if students also have to *read increasingly challenging material independently*.

Consistent with the new curriculum's privileging of formality and accuracy, 'speaking and listening' has been replaced by 'spoken language'. Within this aspect of English, teachers are expected to give due emphasis to succinctness and structure – for example, *giving short speeches and presentations, expressing their own ideas and keeping to the point* – but discussion and drama are still present, and the introduction to 'Spoken language' recognises how speech *continues to underpin the development of pupils' reading and writing* and how the skills of *working collaboratively* remain essential.

How do the changes to Key Stage 2 affect Key Stage 3?

The new curriculum includes an explicit 'Grammar and vocabulary' heading, whose leading requirement is that teachers extend and apply *the grammatical knowledge set out in Appendix 2 to the Key Stage 1 and 2 Programmes of Study*. This statutory appendix is designed to support and guide the expanded detail in the Programmes of Study for KS1–2. Inevitably, this will mean that students will arrive in Year 7 with an increasing knowledge of grammar, and automatic expectations about how that knowledge will be secured, developed and applied in KS3. This is an important consideration for secondary English.

One clear opportunity in KS3 will be focusing on 'grammar in use' – dynamic grammar. This could mean building on the insights offered by programmes such as the primary Talk for Writing programme and Exeter University's *Grammar for Writing*. It will be important, though, for heads of English to consider how secure grammatical knowledge is in their team members. Whether grammar is a good thing or not, teaching it wrongly is disastrous and many English teachers may already have gone beyond the point where they can admit to gaps in their own grammar knowledge.

What this means for English departments

Although the new curriculum is slim, it does pose some challenges – and opportunities. The new curriculum's focus on developing pupils' love of reading will certainly require something more than visits to the library and 'silent reading'. Departments who take this requirement seriously will have to adopt the best approaches available, such as community reading, and ensure that all English teachers become regular readers of teen fiction. Departments will need to ask themselves seriously why pupils don't read for pleasure, and why they should.

And what about the requirement for pupils to *understand increasingly challenging texts*? English departments could just take it for granted that this will be true, but to what extent is this left to chance currently? Can heads of English guarantee that a class reader in a top Year 9 group will be much more challenging than one being read in a middle Year 8 group? And how should we define 'challenging'? The disappearance of level descriptors might exacerbate this problem – although teachers are free to stick to the existing ones.

Perhaps the greatest potential benefit of the new KS3 curriculum is that it might enable departments to design a more exciting and coherent English offer. Ofsted's 2012 report, *Moving English Forward*, complained that *The ending of the [KS3] tests has not led to a re-thinking or re-fashioning of the Key Stage 3 curriculum in many schools. Instead, too many schools have used the freedom available to offer a watered-down set of GCSE units.* Currently, KS3 English schemes of work tend to be fragmented into unrelated topics based on specific assessment focuses. The new curriculum might help departments design English around broad skills that can be constantly revisited and applied in different contexts. These broad skills are defined either in the KS3 Programmes of Study or – perhaps better still – in the 'Aims' that front the English National Curriculum.

Overall, the new National Curriculum might be an ideal opportunity to revisit, revise and renew KS3 English. Given the demands of the KS2 Programmes of Study, it would probably be wise if secondary departments undertook this renewal process in consultation with their KS2 colleagues.

Supporting material

Criteria for assuring high-quality phonic work

The core criteria provide schools with clearly defined key features of an effective, systematic, synthetic phonics programme.

Publishers of products can submit self-assessments and their products to be reviewed against the core criteria by independent evaluators. These publishers should contact the phonics mailbox to request a self-assessment form. They will then need to return the self-assessment form together with two copies of their product. A list of publishers and their self-assessments that have been reviewed as meeting the core criteria are available on the 'Phonics Products and the Self-Assessment Process' page.

Published programmes for phonic work should meet each of the following criteria. Further explanatory notes are offered below.

The programme should:

- present high-quality systematic, synthetic phonic work as the prime approach to decoding print, that is a phonics 'first-and-fast' approach (see note 1)
- enable pupils to start learning phonic knowledge and skills using a systematic, synthetic programme by the age of five, with the expectation that they will be fluent readers having secured word-recognition skills by the end of Key Stage 1 (see note 2)
- be designed for the teaching of discrete, daily sessions progressing from simple to more complex phonic knowledge and skills and covering the major grapheme–phoneme correspondences (see note 3)
- enable pupils' progress to be assessed (see note 4)
- use a multi-sensory approach so that pupils learn variously from simultaneous visual, auditory and kinaesthetic activities, which are designed to secure essential phonic knowledge and skills (see note 5)
- demonstrate that phonemes should be blended, in order, from left to right, 'all through the word' for reading
- demonstrate how words can be segmented into their constituent phonemes for spelling and that this is the reverse of blending phonemes to read words
- ensure pupils apply phonic knowledge and skills as their first approach to reading and spelling even if a word is not completely phonically regular
- ensure that pupils are taught high-frequency words that do not conform completely to grapheme–phoneme correspondence rules
- provide fidelity to the teaching framework for the duration of the programme, to ensure that these irregular words are fully learned (see note 6)
- ensure that as pupils move through the early stages of acquiring phonics, they are invited to practise by reading texts that are entirely decodable for them, so that they experience success and learn to rely on phonemic strategies (see note 7).

Explanatory notes

1. Phonic work is best understood as a body of knowledge and skills about how the alphabet works, rather than one of a range of optional 'methods' or 'strategies' for teaching pupils how to read. For example, phonic programmes should not encourage pupils to guess words from non-phonic clues, such as pictures, before applying phonic knowledge and skills. High-quality systematic, synthetic phonic work will make sure that pupils learn:

   - grapheme–phoneme (letter–sound) correspondences (the alphabetic principle) in a clearly defined, incremental sequence
   - to apply the highly important skill of blending (synthesising) phonemes, in order, all through a word to read it
   - to apply the skills of segmenting words into their constituent phonemes to spell
   - that blending and segmenting are reversible processes.

2. Teachers will make principled, professional judgements about when to start on a systematic, synthetic programme of phonic work but it is reasonable to expect that the great majority of pupils will be capable of, and benefit from, doing so by the age of five. It is equally important for the programme to be designed so that pupils become fluent readers having secured word-recognition skills by the end of Key Stage 1.

3. The programme should introduce a defined initial group of consonants and vowels, enabling pupils, early on, to read and spell many simple CVC words.

4. If the programme is high quality, systematic and synthetic, it will, by design, map incremental progression in phonic knowledge and skills. It should therefore enable teachers to: track pupils' progress; assess for further learning; and identify incipient difficulties so that appropriate support can be provided.

5. Multi-sensory activities should be interesting and engaging but firmly focused on intensifying the learning associated with its phonic goal. They should avoid taking pupils down a circuitous route only tenuously linked to the goal. This means avoiding over-elaborate activities that are difficult to manage and take too long to complete, thus distracting the pupils from concentrating on the learning goal.

6. The programme should not neglect engaging and helpful approaches to the more challenging levels where pupils have to distinguish between phonically irregular graphemes and phonemes.

7. It is important that texts are of the appropriate level for pupils to apply and practise the phonic knowledge and skills that they have learned. Pupils should not be expected to use strategies such as whole-word recognition and/or cues from context, grammar, or pictures.

Example planning

Lower KS2 Text: *The King of the Birds* by Helen Ward

Length of sequence: 3 weeks

Key learning outcome: To write their own *The King of the...* story

Elicitation task: Give pupils an outline of the story: a group of animals meet, they set a competition to decide who will be king, they set off and someone unexpected becomes king. Allow pupils time to talk about their story and develop elements before writing it.

Use the outcomes from this to adapt the *must/should/could* below

All pupils must...	Most pupils should...	Some pupils could...

• include speech marks
• modify nouns
• use commas in lists.
	• use adventurous vocabulary, including expanded noun phrases and alliteration
	• use correct speech punctuation.
		• effectively use some of the stylistic devices in the text such as:
		  • varying the pace
		  • creating patterns
		  • ambitious and apt vocabulary.
		• possible extension to create the key at the end of the book.

Guided group writing targets

Teaching	Guided work linked to sequence	Learning (I can/know/ understand...)

Familiarisation/Immersion in text/Analysis
Imitate
(Learning and remembering, boxing up, book talk, writer talk, sentence level, warming up the word, generating success criteria)
• Imagine that the class is a group of birds and role play making the decision of who will be king.
• Learn and remember the story, *The King of the Birds*, using a map and actions. Retell in groups and pairs, stepping it out side-by-side and in pairs facing each other.
• Retell the story as a class chanting and show the images in the book at the same time. When speech occurs, ask the pupils to hold up a speech bubble to show that they know it is speech.
• Interview the wren about becoming the king. Plan questions and then hot-seat the bird.
• Pick out words and phrases that you like. Write each one on a small piece of paper until you have a large pile of them. Model how to read them and then choose some to put together to create a poem. Complete in small groups, ensuring that the pupils re-read what they have done so far as they create the poem. As groups, perform the poem to the rest of the class.
• Grammar
  • Look at the page with the struggling broad-bellied birds. Create the sentence with pupils each holding a word from it. Ask the other pupils to remove all the extra information so that you are left with just the essential elements. Which words are left in or taken out? (Year 4)
  • Give pupils a range of objects from a group, such as a range of sweets. Create the sentence with sweets instead of birds and now ask the class to see what information they could add. (See below for an example) (Year 4)
  • Retell the story and ask pupils to write the speech in speech bubbles. Show the class that in this story speech bubbles aren't used but inverted commas are. Model how they are used by 'popping' the speech bubble, leaving the inverted commas around the words. Ask pupils to pop the speech bubbles and record the speech without them (Year 3) and with all the punctuation (Year 4).
  • Take the sentence *They flapped, bounded, leapt and lumbered...* and ask the pupils what they notice about it (commas in list, verbs, alliteration, simile). Read again and ask the pupils to use an action when they hear a verb and where the commas should be.
• Box up the story with the pupils (there is an example below the sequence).
Innovate
(Outline innovate task, mirror key activities, boxing up, modelling capturing ideas, shared writing)
• Explain to the class that they are going to create a new story called *The King of the Trees*.
• Visit a group of trees in the school grounds or outside and photograph them in detail: the bark, the leaves, the shape and generate words to describe them. Record these.
• Transform the broad-bellied birds sentence into one about trees, saying it with the correct punctuation. Pupils record it.
• Using the boxing-up chart, transform the ideas from the bird story into the tree story, working out some of the challenges in the story (see italics in the boxing-up chart).
• Complete the rest of the boxes with ideas and then take the story map and start to retell the story, making changes to the map to make it fit the tree theme.
• Model how to write various parts of the story and, individually, invite pupils to write their own version of *The King of the Trees*.
Mark this writing and use the areas for development to focus the teaching in the inventing section.		

Capturing ideas		
Invent (Outline invent task possibilities, learning and remembering own texts, choosing/selecting/organising ideas, boxing up) • Draw up a list of ideas that pupils might write about in their stories: King of the soldiers, dinosaurs, sweets… Allow them to choose one idea. • Using the boxing-up chart, ask the pupils to make notes about what will happen in their story. • With a version of the story map, get pupils to work their way through making changes to it to fit their story. Practise retelling it focusing in on the ways that the group are described at various points. • Individuals tell the story to pupils in another class and ask for their feedback. **Shared writing:** • Model writing the parts of the story that the pupils found more difficult in the innovating section. • Model writing the speech to include inverted commas. • Proofread and edit the story. • Publish the story. • Compare writing in the elicitation task and key learning outcome and describe how the writing has improved.		

Boxing up

Imitate – *The King of the Birds*	Innovate – *The King of the Trees*	Invent
The birds get together to announce that they need to decide who will be king.	*The trees in the woods get together to announce that they need to decide who will be king – north and south trees, light and dark trees, needle and berry trees.*	
They make suggestions about how they will decide.	*It could be the tallest tree, the widest tree, the shiniest tree, the most-berried tree, the fastest-growing tree, the lobed-leaf tree.*	
They decide it will be the bird who can fly the highest and set off.		
The eagle flew the highest and the birds thought that he was the winner but then the wren popped out and flew above the eagle.		
The wren becomes king.		

Medium-term plan (core objectives from PoS)

Reading	Writing	Links to grammar and punctuation appendix
Discussing words and phrases that capture the reader's interest and imagination. Checking that the text makes sense to them, discussing their understanding and explaining the meaning of words in context. Participate in discussion about both books that are read to them and those they can read for themselves, taking turns and listening to what others say.	Plan writing by discussing writing similar to that which they are planning to write in order to understand and learn from its structure, vocabulary and grammar. Draft and write by composing and rehearsing sentences orally, progressively building a varied and rich vocabulary and an increasing range of sentence structures.	Using and punctuating direct speech Noun phrases expanded by addition of modifying adjectives and preposition phrases **Grammar terminology** Verb (building on from Year 2) Inverted commas (Year 3), direct speech (Year 3) Adverb (Year 3), adverbial (Year 4)
Spoken language • Participate in discussions, role play, improvisations. • Use spoken language to develop understanding through imagining and exploring ideas.		

Sentence example

The sweets, the sherbets and lollipops, the toffees and fudge, the jelly beans and the crunchies all rustled louder.

The whistling, lip-smacking sweets, the zinging sherbets and lollipops, the slow melting of the toffees and cream-tasting fudges, the busy feet of jelly beans and the popping of crunchies all rustled louder and louder, a bag of sweets noisily unwrapping themselves.

Example planning

Spelling

Year 3 Statutory requirements

Pupils should be taught to:
- *develop a range of personal strategies for learning new and irregular words*
- *develop a range of personal strategies for spelling at the point of composition*
- *develop a range of strategies for checking and proofreading spellings after writing*
- use further prefixes and suffixes and understand how to add them (English Appendix 1)
- spell further homophones
- spell words that are often misspelled (English Appendix 1)
- place the possessive apostrophe accurately in words with regular plurals [for example, *girls'*, *boys'*] and in words with irregular plurals [for example, *children*]
- use the first two or three letters of a word to check its spelling in a dictionary
- write from memory simple sentences, dictated by the teacher, that include words and punctuation taught so far
- proofread for spelling errors

(Items in italics are non-statutory)

Term 1	Term 2	Term 3
Revisit and review: Common exception words from Year 2. **Prefixes and suffixes:** Revise prefix un-. *(Select from Support for Spelling Unit Y2 T3 i)* New prefixes: pre-, dis-, mis-, re-. Revise suffixes from Year 2: -s, -es, -ed, -ing, -er. *(Spelling Bank pp.4, 6, 7, 8, 18, 23) (Support for Spelling Unit Y2 T1 ii and Unit Y3 T3 ii)* **Teaching rarer GPCs:** Words with the /eɪ/ sound spelled ei, eigh, or ey (ey – th**ey**, ei – v**ei**n, eigh – **eigh**t, aigh – str**aigh**t i – **i**n, y – g**y**m (o – w**o**men, u – b**u**sy, ui – b**ui**ld, e – pr**e**tty) u – **u**p, o – s**o**n, (ou – y**ou**ng, oe – d**oe**s, oo – bl**oo**d) Words ending with the /g/ sound spelled -gue and the /k/ sound spelled -que (French in origin) **Homophones:** brake/break, grate/great, eight/ate, weight/wait, son/sun *(Support for Spelling Unit Y4 T1 i)* **Apostrophe:** Revise contractions from Year 2, eg can't, didn't. *(Support for Spelling Unit Y4 T3 i and Spelling Bank pp.15, 19)* **Proofreading: Focus:** checking after writing spelling of KS1 common exception/tricky words.	**Revisit and review:** Suffixes from Year 2: -ment, -ness, -ful, -less, -ly (with a consonant before it) *(Spelling Bank p.14)* **Prefixes and suffixes:** Prefixes: sub-, tele-, super-, auto-. *(Support for Spelling Unit Y2 T2 ii and Unit Y4 T3 ii)* **Teaching rarer GPCs:** Words with the /ʃ/ sound spelled ch (mostly French in origin), eg chef. sh – **sh**op, s – **s**ure, ss – mi**ss**ion ('t' before 'ion' – mention, ci – spe**ci**al, 't' before 'ial' – par**ti**al, ch – **ch**ef, ce – o**ce**an) Words with the /k/ sound spelled ch (Greek in origin), eg scheme, chorus, chemist, echo, character **Homophones:** here/hear, knot/not, meat/meet, missed/mist. *(Support for Spelling Unit Y4 T1 i)* **Apostrophe:** Revise contractions from Year 2, eg hasn't, couldn't. *(Support for Spelling Unit Y4 T3 i)* *(Spelling Bank pp. 15, 19)* **Proofreading:** Using a dictionary to check spellings. First two letters.	**Revisit and review:** Revise strategies for spelling at the point of writing. **Prefixes and suffixes:**.Suffix -ly straight on to root word, eg sadly, unusually. *(Support for Spelling Unit Y3 T2 ii, Spelling Bank pp. 13, 14)* **Teaching rarer GPCs:** The /ʌ/ sound spelled ou, eg young, touch. The /ɪ/ sound spelled y elsewhere than at the end of words, eg gym, myth. **Homophones:** heel/heal/he'll, plain/plane, berry/bury, groan/grown, rain/rein/reign. Also homophones from Year 3/4 word list: heard/herd, through/threw, *(Support for Spelling Unit Y4 T1 i)* **Apostrophe:** Revise contractions from Year 2, eg it's, I'll. *(Support for Spelling Unit Y4 T3 i) (Spelling Bank pp. 15, 19, 37)* **Proofreading:** Proofread own writing for misspellings of personal spelling list words.
Learning spellings *(Spelling Bank p.16)* Pupils: • Learn words taught in new knowledge this term. • Learn words from Years 3/4 word list. Suggest an average of 5/6 a term of highlighted words. Group other words for cross-curricular teaching. • Learn words from personal list. **Extend the knowledge of spelling strategies and apply to high-frequency and cross-curricular words from Years 3/4 word list groups.**	**Learning spellings** *(Spelling Bank p.16* Pupils: • Learn words taught in new knowledge this term. • Learn words from Years 3/4 word list. Suggest an average of 5/6 a term of highlighted words. **Teach: February** Group other words for cross-curricular teaching. • Learn words from personal list. **Extend the knowledge of spelling strategies and apply to high-frequency and cross-curricular words from Years 3/4 word list groups.**	**Learning spellings** *(Spelling Bank p.16* Pupils: • Learn words taught in new knowledge this term. • Learn words from Years 3/4 word list. Suggest an average of 5/6 a term of highlighted words. Group other words for cross-curricular teaching. • Learn words from personal list. **Extend the knowledge of spelling strategies and apply to high-frequency and cross-curricular words from Years 3/4 word list groups.**

Example planning

Spelling (continued)

Year 3: Term 2, 1st half term					
Week 1	**Week 2**	**Week 3**	**Week 4**	**Week 5**	**Week 6**
Revisit/review -ness and -ful (with consonant before it)		**Revise** Apostrophe for contractions *hasn't, didn't*		**Apply** Dictation using words with /ʃ/ in	
	Practise Prefixes sub- and tele-		**Teach** /ʃ/ spelled ch – *chef*, sh – *shop*, s – *sure*, ss – *mission*, ci – *special*		**Practise** Suffixes -less and -ly after a consonant
Practise spelling words with suffixes: -ness and -ful		**Learn** new words from personal spelling list and statutory list		**Learn** new words from personal spelling list and statutory list	
	Apply Prefixes sub- and tele-		Practise /ʃ/		**Apply** Suffixes -less and -ly after a consonant
Teach Prefixes sub- and tele-		**Apply** learned words Pair testing		**Teach** Suffixes -less and -ly after a consonant	

National Curriculum: Key Stages 1–2

1. Introduction

1.1 This document sets out the framework for the National Curriculum at Key Stages 1 and 2, and includes:

- contextual information about both the overall school curriculum and the statutory National Curriculum, including the statutory basis of the latter
- aims for the statutory National Curriculum
- statements on inclusion, and on the development of pupils' competence in numeracy and mathematics, language and literacy across the school curriculum
- Programmes of Study for all the National Curriculum subjects that are taught at Key Stages 1 and 2.

2. The school curriculum in England

2.1 Every state-funded school must offer a curriculum which is balanced and broadly based[1] and which:

- promotes the spiritual, moral, cultural, mental and physical development of pupils at the school and of society, and
- prepares pupils at the school for the opportunities, responsibilities and experiences of later life.

2.2 The school curriculum comprises all learning and other experiences that each school plans for its pupils. The National Curriculum forms one part of the school curriculum.

2.3 All state schools are also required to make provision for a daily act of collective worship and must teach religious education to pupils at every key stage and sex and relationship education to pupils in secondary education.

2.4 Maintained schools in England are legally required to follow the statutory National Curriculum which sets out in Programmes of Study, on the basis of key stages, subject content for those subjects that should be taught to all pupils. All schools must publish their school curriculum by subject and academic year online.[2]

2.5 All schools should make provision for personal, social, health and economic education (PSHE), drawing on good practice. Schools are also free to include other subjects or topics of their choice in planning and designing their own programme of education.

---

[1] See Section 78 of the 2002 Education Act: http://www.legislation.gov.uk/ukpga/2002/32/section/78 which applies to all maintained schools. Academies are also required to offer a broad and balanced curriculum in accordance with Section 1 of the 2010 Academies Act: http://www.legislation.gov.uk/ukpga/2010/32/section/1

[2] From September 2012, all schools are required to publish information in relation to each academic year, relating to the content of the school's curriculum for each subject and details about how additional information relating to the curriculum may be obtained: http://www.legislation.gov.uk/uksi/2012/1124/made.

3. The National Curriculum in England

Aims

3.1 The National Curriculum provides pupils with an introduction to the essential knowledge that they need to be educated citizens. It introduces pupils to the best that has been thought and said, and helps engender an appreciation of human creativity and achievement.

3.2 The National Curriculum is just one element in the education of every child. There is time and space in the school day and in each week, term and year to range beyond the National Curriculum specifications. The National Curriculum provides an outline of core knowledge around which teachers can develop exciting and stimulating lessons to promote the development of pupils' knowledge, understanding and skills as part of the wider school curriculum.

Structure

3.3 Pupils of compulsory school age in community and foundation schools, including community special schools and foundation special schools, and in voluntary aided and voluntary controlled schools, must follow the National Curriculum. It is organised on the basis of four key stages[3] and twelve subjects, classified in legal terms as 'core' and 'other foundation' subjects.

3.4 The Secretary of State for Education is required to publish Programmes of Study for each National Curriculum subject, setting out the 'matters, skills and processes' to be taught at each key stage. Schools are free to choose how they organise their school day, as long as the content of National Curriculum Programmes of Study is taught to all pupils.

---

[3] The Key Stage 2 Programmes of Study for English, mathematics and science are presented in this document as 'lower' (Years 3 and 4) and 'upper' (Years 5 and 6). This distinction is made as guidance for teachers and is not reflected in legislation. The legal requirement is to cover the content of the Programmes of Study for Years 3 to 6 by the end of Key Stage 2.

3.5 The proposed structure of the new National Curriculum, in terms of which subjects are compulsory at each key stage, is set out in the table below.

Figure 1 – Structure of the National Curriculum

	Key Stage 1	Key Stage 2	Key Stage 3	Key Stage 4
Age	5–7	7–11	11–14	14–16
Year groups	1–2	3–6	7–9	10–11
Core subjects				
English	✓	✓	✓	✓
Mathematics	✓	✓	✓	✓
Science	✓	✓	✓	✓
Foundation subjects				
Art and design	✓	✓	✓	
Citizenship			✓	✓
Computing	✓	✓	✓	✓
Design and technology	✓	✓	✓	
Languages[4]		✓	✓	
Geography	✓	✓	✓	
History	✓	✓	✓	
Music	✓	✓	✓	
Physical education	✓	✓	✓	✓

3.6 All schools are also required to teach religious education at all key stages.

Secondary schools must provide sex and relationship education.

Figure 2 – Statutory teaching of religious education and sex and relationship education

	Key Stage 1	Key Stage 2	Key Stage 3	Key Stage 4
Age	5–7	7–11	11–14	14–16
Year groups	1–2	3–6	7–9	10–11
Religious education	✓	✓	✓	✓
Sex and relationship education			✓	✓

---

[4] At Key Stage 2 the subject title is 'foreign language'; at Key Stage 3 it is 'modern foreign language'.

4. Inclusion

Setting suitable challenges

4.1 Teachers should set high expectations for every pupil. They should plan stretching work for children whose attainment is significantly above the expected standard. They have an even greater obligation to plan lessons for pupils who have low levels of prior attainment or come from disadvantaged backgrounds. Teachers should use appropriate assessment to set targets which are deliberately ambitious.

Responding to pupils' needs and overcoming potential barriers for individuals and groups of pupils

4.2 Teachers should take account of their duties under equal opportunities legislation[5] that covers race, disability, sex, religion or belief, sexual orientation, pregnancy and maternity, and gender assessment.

4.3 A wide range of pupils have special educational needs, many of whom also have disabilities. Lessons should be planned to ensure that there are no barriers to every child achieving. In many cases, such planning will mean that these pupils will be able to study the full National Curriculum. The SEN Code of Practice will include advice on approaches to identification of need which can support this. A minority of pupils will need access to specialist equipment and different approaches. The SEN Code of Practice will outline what needs to be done for them.

4.4 With the right teaching that recognises their individual needs, many disabled pupils have little need for additional resources beyond the aids which they use as part of their daily life. Teachers must plan lessons so that these pupils can study every National Curriculum subject. Potential areas of difficulty should be identified and addressed at the outset of work.

4.5 Teachers must also take account of the needs of pupils whose first language is not English. Monitoring of progress should take account of the child's age, length of time in this country, previous educational experience and ability in other languages.

4.6 The ability of pupils for whom English is an additional language to take part in the National Curriculum may be in advance of their communication skills in English. Teachers should plan teaching opportunities to help pupils develop their English and should aim to provide the support pupils need to take part in all subjects.

---

[5] Age is a protected characteristic under the Equality Act 2010 but it is not applicable to schools in relation to education or (as far as relating to those under the age of 18) the provision of services; it is a relevant protected characteristic in relation to the provision of services or employment (so when thinking about staff). Marriage and civil partnership are also a protected characteristic but only in relation to employment.

5. Numeracy and mathematics

5.1 Teachers should use every relevant subject to develop pupils' mathematical fluency. Confidence in numeracy and other mathematical skills is a precondition of success across the National Curriculum

5.2 Teachers should develop pupils' numeracy and mathematical reasoning in all subjects so that they understand and appreciate the importance of mathematics. Pupils should be taught to apply arithmetic fluently to problems, understand and use measures, make estimates and sense check their work. Pupils should apply their geometric and algebraic understanding, and relate their understanding of probability to the notions of risk and uncertainty. They should also understand the cycle of collecting, presenting and analysing data. They should be taught to apply their mathematics to both routine and non-routine problems, including breaking down more complex problems into a series of simpler steps.

6. Language and literacy

6.1 Teachers should develop pupils' spoken language, reading, writing and vocabulary as integral aspects of the teaching of every subject. English is both a subject in its own right and the medium for teaching; for pupils, understanding the language provides access to the whole curriculum. Fluency in the English language is an essential foundation for success in all subjects.

Spoken language

6.2 Pupils should be taught to speak clearly and convey ideas confidently using Standard English. They should learn to justify ideas with reasons; ask questions to check understanding; develop vocabulary and build knowledge; negotiate; evaluate and build on the ideas of others; and select the appropriate register for effective communication. They should be taught to give well-structured descriptions and explanations and develop their understanding through speculating, hypothesising and exploring ideas. This will enable them to clarify their thinking as well as organise their ideas for writing.

Reading and writing

6.3 Teachers should develop pupils' reading and writing in all subjects to support their acquisition of knowledge. Pupils should be taught to read fluently, understand extended prose (both fiction and non-fiction) and be encouraged to read for pleasure. Schools should do everything to promote wider reading. They should provide library facilities and set ambitious expectations for reading at home. Pupils should develop the stamina and skills to write at length, with accurate spelling and punctuation. They should be taught the correct use of grammar. They should build on what they have been taught to expand the range of their writing and the variety of the grammar they use. The writing they do should include narratives, explanations, descriptions, comparisons, summaries and evaluations: such writing supports them in rehearsing, understanding and consolidating what they have heard or read.

Vocabulary development

6.4 Pupils' acquisition and command of vocabulary are key to their learning and progress across the whole curriculum. Teachers should therefore develop vocabulary actively, building systematically on pupils' current knowledge. They should increase pupils' store of words in general; simultaneously, they should also make links between known and new vocabulary and discuss the shades of meaning in similar words. In this way, pupils expand the vocabulary choices that are available to them when they write. In addition, it is vital for pupils' comprehension that they understand the meanings of words they meet in their reading across all subjects, and older pupils should be taught the meaning of instruction verbs that they may meet in examination questions. It is particularly important to induct pupils into the language which defines each subject in its own right, such as accurate mathematical and scientific language.

7. Programmes of Study and Attainment targets

7.1 The following pages set out the proposed statutory Programmes of Study for all subjects at Key Stages 1–2. Where content is shown in grey text, it is 'non-statutory'.

SCHOLASTIC

English Programme of Study: KS1–2

Purpose of study

English has a pre-eminent place in education and in society. A high-quality education in English will teach pupils to write and speak fluently so that they can communicate their ideas and emotions to others and through their reading and listening, others can communicate with them. Through reading in particular, pupils have a chance to develop culturally, emotionally, intellectually, socially and spiritually. Literature, especially, plays a key role in such development. Reading also enables pupils both to acquire knowledge and to build on what they already know. All the skills of language are essential to participating fully as a member of society; pupils, therefore, who do not learn to speak, read and write fluently and confidently are effectively disenfranchised.

Aims

The overarching aim for English in the National Curriculum is to promote high standards of literacy by equipping pupils with a strong command of the spoken and written word, and to develop their love of literature through widespread reading for enjoyment. The National Curriculum for English aims to ensure that all pupils:

- read easily, fluently and with good understanding
- develop the habit of reading widely and often, for both pleasure and information
- acquire a wide vocabulary, an understanding of grammar and knowledge of linguistic conventions for reading, writing and spoken language
- appreciate our rich and varied literary heritage
- write clearly, accurately and coherently, adapting their language and style in and for a range of contexts, purposes and audiences
- use discussion in order to learn; they should be able to elaborate and explain clearly their understanding and ideas
- are competent in the arts of speaking and listening, making formal presentations, demonstrating to others and participating in debate.

Spoken language

The National Curriculum for English reflects the importance of spoken language in pupils' development across the whole curriculum – cognitively, socially and linguistically. Spoken language underpins the development of reading and writing. The quality and variety of language that pupils hear and speak are vital for developing their vocabulary and grammar and their understanding for reading and writing. Teachers should therefore ensure the continual development of pupils' confidence and competence in spoken language and listening skills.

Pupils should develop a capacity to explain their understanding of books and other reading, and to prepare their ideas before they write. They must be assisted in making their thinking clear to themselves as well as to others and teachers should ensure that pupils build secure foundations by using discussion to probe and remedy their misconceptions. Pupils should also be taught to understand and use the conventions for discussion and debate.

All pupils should be enabled to participate in and gain knowledge, skills and understanding associated with the artistic practice of drama. Pupils should be able to adopt, create and sustain a range of roles, responding appropriately to others in role. They should have opportunities to improvise, devise and script drama for one another and a range of audiences, as well as to rehearse, refine, share and respond thoughtfully to drama and theatre performances.

Statutory requirements which underpin all aspects of speaking and listening across the six years of primary education form part of the National Curriculum. These are reflected and contextualised within the reading and writing Domains which follow.

Reading

The Programmes of Study for reading at Key Stages 1 and 2 consist of two dimensions:

- word reading
- comprehension (both listening and reading).

It is essential that teaching focuses on developing pupils' competence in both dimensions; different kinds of teaching are needed for each.

Skilled word reading involves both the speedy working out of the pronunciation of unfamiliar printed words (decoding) and the speedy recognition of familiar printed words. Underpinning both is the understanding that the letters on the page represent the sounds in spoken words. This is why phonics should be emphasised in the early teaching of reading to beginners (that is, unskilled readers) when they start school.

Good comprehension draws from linguistic knowledge (in particular of vocabulary and grammar) and on knowledge of the world. Comprehension skills develop through pupils' experience of high-quality discussion with the teacher, as well as from reading and discussing a range of stories, poems and non-fiction. All pupils must be encouraged to read widely across both fiction and non-fiction to develop their knowledge of themselves and the world in which they live, to establish an appreciation and love of reading, and to gain knowledge across the curriculum. Reading widely and often increases pupils' vocabulary because they encounter words they would rarely hear or use in everyday speech. Reading also feeds pupils' imagination and opens up a treasure-house of wonder and joy for curious young minds.

It is essential that, by the end of their primary education, all pupils are able to read fluently, and with confidence, in any subject in their forthcoming secondary education.

Writing

The Programmes of Study for writing at Key Stages 1 and 2 are constructed similarly to those for reading:

- transcription (spelling and handwriting)
- composition (articulating ideas and structuring them in speech and writing).

It is essential that teaching develops pupils' competence in these two dimensions. In addition, pupils should be taught how to plan, revise and evaluate their writing. These aspects of writing have been incorporated into the Programmes of Study for composition.

Writing down ideas fluently depends on effective transcription: that is, on spelling quickly and accurately through knowing the relationship between sounds and letters (phonics) and understanding the morphology (word structure) and orthography (spelling structure) of words. Effective composition involves articulating and communicating ideas, and then organising them coherently for a reader. This requires clarity, awareness of the audience, purpose and context, and an increasingly wide knowledge of vocabulary and grammar. Writing also depends on fluent, legible and, eventually, speedy handwriting.

Spelling, vocabulary, grammar, punctuation and glossary

The two statutory appendices – on spelling and on vocabulary, grammar and punctuation – give an overview of the specific features that should be included in teaching the Programme of Study.

Opportunities for teachers to enhance pupils' vocabulary arise naturally from their reading and writing. As vocabulary increases, teachers should show pupils how to understand the relationships between words, how to understand nuances in meaning, and how to develop their understanding of, and ability to use, figurative language. They should also teach pupils how to work out and clarify the meanings of unknown words and words with more than one meaning. References to developing pupils' vocabulary are also included within the appendices.

Pupils should be taught to control their speaking and writing consciously and to use Standard English. They should be taught to use the elements of spelling, grammar, punctuation and 'language about language' listed. This is not intended to constrain or restrict teachers' creativity, but simply to provide the structure on which they can construct exciting lessons. A non-statutory glossary is provided for teachers. Throughout the Programme of Study, teachers should teach pupils the vocabulary they need to discuss their reading, writing and spoken language. It is important that pupils learn the correct grammatical terms in English and that these terms are integrated within teaching.

School curriculum

The Programmes of Study for English are set out year by year for Key Stage 1 and two-yearly for Key Stage 2. The single-year blocks at Key Stage 1 reflect the rapid pace of development in word reading during these two years. Schools are, however, only required to teach the relevant Programme of Study by the end of the key stage. Within each key stage, schools therefore have the flexibility to introduce content earlier or later than set out in the Programme of Study. In addition, schools can introduce content during an earlier key stage if appropriate.

All schools are also required to set out their school curriculum for English on a year-by-year basis and make this information available online.

Attainment targets

By the end of each key stage, pupils are expected to know, apply and understand the matters, skills and processes specified in the relevant Programme of Study.

Schools are not required by law to teach the example content in grey or the content indicated as being 'non-statutory'.

English Programme of Study: Spoken language – Years 1–6

Programme of Study (statutory requirements)	Notes and guidance (non-statutory)
SPOKEN LANGUAGE	**SPOKEN LANGUAGE**
Pupils should be taught to:	These statements apply to all years. The content should be taught at a level appropriate to the age of the pupils. Pupils should build on the oral language skills that have been taught in preceding years.
• listen and respond appropriately to adults and their peers	
• ask relevant questions to extend their understanding and knowledge	Pupils should be taught to develop their competence in spoken language and listening to enhance the effectiveness with which they are able to communicate across a range of contexts and to a range of audiences. They should therefore have opportunities to work in groups of different sizes – in pairs, small, large groups and as a whole class.
• use relevant strategies to build their vocabulary	
• articulate and justify answers, arguments and opinions	
• give well-structured descriptions, explanations and narratives for different purposes, including for expressing feelings	Pupils should understand how to take turns and when and how to participate constructively in conversations and debates.
• maintain attention and participate actively in collaborative conversations, staying on topic and initiating and responding to comments	Attention should also be paid to increasing pupils' vocabulary, ranging from describing their immediate world and feelings to developing a broader, deeper and richer vocabulary to discuss abstract concepts and a wider range of topics, and to their knowledge about language as a whole.
• use spoken language to develop understanding through speculating, hypothesising, imagining and exploring ideas	
• speak audibly and fluently with an increasing command of Standard English	
• participate in discussions, presentations, performances, role play, improvisations and debates	Pupils should receive constructive feedback on their spoken language and listening not only to improve their knowledge and skills but also to establish secure foundations for effective spoken language in their studies at primary school, helping them to achieve in secondary education and beyond.
• gain, maintain and monitor the interest of the listener(s)	
• consider and evaluate different viewpoints, attending to and building on the contributions of others	
• select and use appropriate registers for effective communication.	

Key Stage 1

Year 1

During Year 1, teachers should build on work from the Early Years Foundation Stage, making sure that pupils can sound and blend unfamiliar printed words quickly and accurately using the phonic knowledge and skills that they have already learned. Teachers should also ensure that pupils continue to learn new grapheme–phoneme correspondences (GPCs) and revise and consolidate those learned earlier. The understanding that the letter(s) on the page represent the sounds in spoken words should underpin pupils' reading and spelling of all words. This includes common words containing unusual GPCs. The term 'common exception words' is used throughout the Programmes of Study for such words.

Alongside this knowledge of GPCs, pupils need to develop the skill of blending the sounds into words for reading and establish the habit of applying this skill whenever they encounter new words. This will be supported by practising their reading with books consistent with their developing phonic knowledge and skill and their knowledge of common exception words. At the same time they will need to hear, share and discuss a wide range of high-quality books to develop a love of reading and broaden their vocabulary.

Pupils should be helped to read words without overt sounding and blending after a few encounters. Those who are slow to develop this skill should have extra practice.

Pupils' writing during Year 1 will generally develop at a slower pace than their reading. This is because they need to encode the sounds they hear in words (spelling skills), develop the physical skill needed for handwriting, and learn how to organise their ideas in writing.

Pupils entering Year 1 who have not yet met the early learning goals for literacy should continue to follow their school's curriculum or the Early Years Foundation Stage to develop their word reading, spelling and language skills. However, these pupils should follow the Year 1 Programme of Study in terms of the books they listen to and discuss, so that they develop their vocabulary and understanding of grammar, as well as their knowledge more generally across the curriculum. If they are still struggling to decode and spell, they need to be taught to do this urgently through a rigorous and systematic phonics programme so that they catch up rapidly.

Teachers should ensure that their teaching develops pupils' oral vocabulary as well as their ability to understand and use a variety of grammatical structures, giving particular support to pupils whose oral language skills are insufficiently developed.

Year 1 Programme of Study (statutory requirements)	Notes and guidance (non-statutory)
READING **Word reading** Pupils should be taught to: • apply phonic knowledge and skills as the route to decode words • respond speedily with the correct sound to graphemes (letters or groups of letters) for all 40+ phonemes, including, where applicable, alternative sounds for graphemes • read accurately by blending sounds in unfamiliar words containing GPCs that have been taught • read common exception words, noting unusual correspondences between spelling and sound and where these occur in the word • read words containing taught GPCs and -s, -es, -ing, -ed, -er and -est endings • read other words of more than one syllable that contain taught GPCs • read words with contractions, (for example *I'm, I'll, we'll*), and understand that the apostrophe represents the omitted letter(s) • read aloud accurately books that are consistent with their developing phonic knowledge and that do not require them to use other strategies to work out words • re-read these books to build up their fluency and confidence in word reading.	**READING** **Word reading** Pupils should revise and consolidate the GPCs and the common exception words taught in Reception. As soon as they can read words comprising the Year 1 GPCs accurately and speedily, they should move on to the Year 2 Programme of Study for word reading. The number, order and choice of exception words taught will vary according to the phonics programme being used. Ensuring that pupils are aware of the GPCs they contain, however unusual these are, supports spelling later. Young readers encounter words that they have not seen before much more frequently than experienced readers do, and they may not know the meaning of some of these. Practice at reading such words by sounding and blending can provide opportunities not only for pupils to develop confidence in their decoding skills, but also for teachers to explain the meaning and thus develop pupils' vocabulary. Pupils should be taught how to read words with suffixes by being helped to build on the root words that they can read already. Pupils' reading and re-reading of books that are closely matched to their developing phonic knowledge and knowledge of common exception words supports their fluency, as well as increasing their confidence in their reading skills. Fluent word reading greatly assists comprehension, especially when pupils come to read longer books.

Year 1 Programme of Study (statutory requirements)	Notes and guidance (non-statutory)
READING	**READING**
Comprehension	**Comprehension**
Pupils should be taught to:	Pupils should have extensive experience of listening to, sharing and discussing a wide range of high-quality books with the teacher, other adults and each other to engender a love of reading at the same time as they are reading independently.
• develop pleasure in reading, motivation to read, vocabulary and understanding by:	
• listening to and discussing a wide range of poems, stories and non-fiction at a level beyond that at which they can read independently	Pupils' vocabulary should be developed when they listen to books read aloud and when they discuss what they have heard. Such vocabulary can also feed into their writing. Knowing the meaning of more words increases pupils' chances of understanding when they read by themselves. The meaning of some new words should be introduced to pupils before they start to read on their own, so that these unknown words do not hold up their comprehension.
• being encouraged to link what they read or hear read to their own experiences	
• becoming very familiar with key stories, fairy stories and traditional tales, retelling them and considering their particular characteristics	
• recognising and joining in with predictable phrases	However, once pupils have already decoded words successfully, the meaning of those that are new to them can be discussed with them, so contributing to developing their early skills of inference. By listening frequently to stories, poems and non-fiction that they cannot yet read for themselves, pupils begin to understand how written language can be structured in order, for example, how to build surprise in narratives or to present facts in non-fiction. Listening to and discussing information books and other non-fiction establishes the foundations for their learning in other subjects. Pupils should be shown some of the processes for finding out information.
• learning to appreciate rhymes and poems, and to recite some by heart	
• discussing word meanings, linking new meanings to those already known	
• understand both the books they can already read accurately and fluently and those they listen to by:	
• drawing on what they already know or on background information and vocabulary provided by the teacher	Through listening, pupils also start to learn how language sounds and increase their vocabulary and awareness of grammatical structures. In due course, they will be able to draw on such grammar in their own writing.
• checking that the text makes sense to them as they read and correcting inaccurate reading	
• discussing the significance of the title and events	Rules for effective discussions should be agreed with and demonstrated for children. They should help to develop and evaluate them, with the expectation that everyone takes part. Pupils should be helped to consider the opinions of others.
• making inferences on the basis of what is being said and done	
• predicting what might happen on the basis of what has been read so far	
• participate in discussion about what is read to them, taking turns and listening to what others say	Role play can help pupils to identify with and explore characters and to try out the language they have listened to.
• explain clearly their understanding of what is read to them.	

Year 1 Programme of Study (statutory requirements)	Notes and guidance (non-statutory)
WRITING	**WRITING**
Transcription	**Transcription**
Spelling (see English Appendix 1)	*Spelling*
Pupils should be taught to:	Reading should be taught alongside spelling, so that pupils understand that they can read back words they have spelt.
• spell:	
• words containing each of the 40+ phonemes already taught	Pupils should be shown how to segment words into individual phonemes and then how to represent the phonemes by the appropriate grapheme(s). It is important to recognise that phoneme–grapheme correspondences (which underpin spelling) are more variable than grapheme–phoneme correspondences (which underpin reading). For this reason, pupils need to do much more word-specific rehearsal for spelling than for reading.
• common exception words	
• the days of the week	
• name the letters of the alphabet:	
• naming the letters of the alphabet in order	
• using letter names to distinguish between alternative spellings of the same sound	At this stage pupils will be spelling some words in a phonically plausible way, even if sometimes incorrectly. Misspellings of words that pupils have been taught to spell should be corrected; other misspelt words should be used to teach pupils about alternative ways of representing those sounds.
• add prefixes and suffixes:	
• using the spelling rule for adding -s or -es as the plural marker for nouns and the third person singular marker for verbs	Writing simple dictated sentences that include words taught so far gives pupils opportunities to apply and practise their spelling.
• using the prefix *un–*	
• using *-ing*, *-ed*, *-er* and *-est* where no change is needed in the spelling of root words (for example, *helping, helped, helper, eating, quicker, quickest*)	
• apply simple spelling rules and guidelines, as listed in English Appendix 1	
• write from memory simple sentences dictated by the teacher that include words using the GPCs and common exception words taught so far.	

Year 1 Programme of Study (statutory requirements)	Notes and guidance (non-statutory)
Handwriting Pupils should be taught to: • sit correctly at a table, holding a pencil comfortably and correctly • begin to form lower-case letters in the correct direction, starting and finishing in the right place • form capital letters • form digits 0–9 • understand which letters belong to which handwriting 'families' (ie letters that are formed in similar ways) and to practise these.	*Handwriting* Handwriting requires frequent and discrete, direct teaching. Pupils should be able to form letters correctly and confidently. The size of the writing implement (pencil, pen) should not be too large for a young child's hand. Whatever is being used should allow the child to hold it easily and correctly so that bad habits are avoided. Left-handed pupils should receive specific teaching to meet their needs.
Composition Pupils should be taught to: • write sentences by: • saying out loud what they are going to write about • composing a sentence orally before writing it • sequencing sentences to form short narratives • re-reading what they have written to check that it makes sense • discuss what they have written with the teacher or other pupils • read aloud their writing clearly enough to be heard by their peers and the teacher.	**Composition** At the beginning of Year 1, not all pupils will have the spelling and handwriting skills they need to write down everything that they can compose out loud. Pupils should understand, through demonstration, the skills and processes essential to writing: that is, thinking aloud as they collect ideas, drafting and re-reading to check their meaning is clear.

Year 1 Programme of Study (statutory requirements)

Vocabulary, grammar and punctuation

Pupils should be taught to:

- develop their understanding of the concepts set out in English Appendix 2 by:

  - leaving spaces between words

  - joining words and joining sentences using *and*

  - beginning to punctuate sentences using a capital letter and a full stop, question mark or exclamation mark

  - using a capital letter for names of people, places, the days of the week, and the personal pronoun 'I'

- learning the grammar for Year 1 in English Appendix 2 in

- use the grammatical terminology in English Appendix 2 in discussing their writing.

Notes and guidance (non-statutory)

Vocabulary, grammar and punctuation

Pupils should be taught to recognise sentence boundaries in spoken sentences and to use the vocabulary listed in English Appendix 2 ('Terminology for pupils') when their writing is discussed.

Pupils should begin to use some of the distinctive features of Standard English in their writing. 'Standard English' is defined in the Glossary.

Year 2

By the beginning of Year 2, pupils should be able to read all common graphemes. They should be able to read unfamiliar words containing these graphemes, accurately and without undue hesitation, by sounding them out in books that are matched closely to each child's level of word reading knowledge. They should also be able to read many common words containing GPCs taught so far, for example, *shout, hand, stop,* or *dream*, without needing to blend the sounds out loud first. Pupils' reading of common exception words, for example, *you, could, many,* or *people*, should be secure. Pupils will increase their fluency by being able to read these words easily and automatically. Finally, pupils should be able to retell some familiar stories that have been read to and discussed with them or that they have acted out during Year 1.

During Year 2, teachers should continue to focus on establishing pupils' accurate and speedy word-reading skills. They should also make sure that pupils listen to and discuss a wide range of stories, poems, plays and information books; this should include whole books. The sooner that pupils can read well and do so frequently, the sooner they will be able to increase their vocabulary, comprehension and their knowledge across the wider curriculum.

In writing, pupils at the beginning of Year 2 should be able to compose individual sentences orally and then write them down. They should be able to spell correctly many of the words covered in Year 1 (see English Appendix 1). They should also be able to make phonically plausible attempts to spell words they have not yet learned. Finally, they should be able to form individual letters correctly, so establishing good handwriting habits from the beginning.

It is important to recognise that pupils begin to meet extra challenges in terms of spelling during Year 2. Increasingly, they should learn that there is not always an obvious connection between the way a word is said and the way it is spelt. Variations include different ways of spelling the same sound, the use of so-called silent letters and groups of letters in some words and, sometimes, spelling that has become separated from the way that words are now pronounced, such as the *-le* ending in *table*. Pupils' motor skills also need to be sufficiently advanced for them to write down ideas that they may be able to compose orally. In addition, writing is intrinsically harder than reading: pupils are likely to be able to read and understand more complex writing (in terms of its vocabulary and structure) than they are capable of producing themselves.

For pupils who do not have the phonic knowledge and skills they need for Year 2, teachers should use the Year 1 Programmes of Study for word reading and spelling so that pupils' word reading skills catch up. However, teachers should use the Year 2 Programme of Study for comprehension so that these pupils hear and talk about new books, poems, other writing and vocabulary with the rest of the class.

Year 2 Programme of Study (statutory requirements)

READING

Word reading

Pupils should be taught to:

- continue to apply phonic knowledge and skills as the route to decode words until automatic decoding has become embedded and reading is fluent
- read accurately by blending the sounds in words that contain the graphemes taught so far, especially recognising alternative sounds for graphemes
- read accurately words of two or more syllables that contain the same graphemes as above
- read words containing common suffixes
- read further common exception words, noting unusual correspondence between spelling and sound and where these occur in the word
- read most words quickly and accurately, without overt sounding and blending, when they have been frequently encountered
- read aloud books closely matched to their improving phonic knowledge, sounding out unfamiliar words accurately, automatically and without undue hesitation
- re-read these books to build up their fluency and confidence in word reading.

Notes and guidance (non-statutory)

READING

Word reading

Pupils should revise and consolidate the GPCs and the common exception words taught in Year 1. The exception words taught will vary slightly, depending on the phonics programme being used. As soon as pupils can read words comprising the Year 2 GPCs accurately and speedily, they should move on to the Years 3 and 4 Programme of Study for word reading.

When pupils are taught how to read longer words, they should be shown syllable boundaries and how to read each syllable separately before they combine them to read the word.

Pupils should be taught how to read suffixes by building on the root words that they have already learned. The whole suffix should be taught as well as the letters that make it up.

Pupils who are still at the early stages of learning to read should have ample practice in reading books that are closely matched to their developing phonic knowledge and knowledge of common exception words. As soon as the decoding of most regular words and common exception words is embedded fully, the range of books that pupils can read independently will expand rapidly. Pupils should have opportunities to exercise choice in selecting books and be taught how to do so.

Year 2 Programme of Study (statutory requirements)

READING

Comprehension

Pupils should be taught to:

- develop pleasure in reading, motivation to read, vocabulary and understanding by:
  - listening to, discussing and expressing views about a wide range of contemporary and classic poetry, stories and non-fiction at a level beyond that at which they can read independently
  - discussing the sequence of events in books and how items of information are related
  - becoming increasingly familiar with and retelling a wider range of stories, fairy stories and traditional tales
  - being introduced to non-fiction books that are structured in different ways
  - recognising simple recurring literary language in stories and poetry
  - discussing and clarifying the meanings of words, linking new meanings to known vocabulary
  - discussing their favourite words and phrases
  - continuing to build up a repertoire of poems learned by heart, appreciating these and reciting some, with appropriate intonation to make the meaning clear
- understand both the books that they can already read accurately and fluently and those that they listen to by:
  - drawing on what they already know or on background information and vocabulary provided by the teacher
  - checking that the text makes sense to them as they read and correcting inaccurate reading
  - making inferences on the basis of what is being said and done
  - answering and asking questions
  - predicting what might happen on the basis of what has been read so far

Notes and guidance (non-statutory)

READING

Comprehension

Pupils should be encouraged to read all the words in a sentence and to do this accurately, so that their understanding of what they read is not hindered by imprecise decoding, for example, by reading 'place' instead of 'palace'.

Pupils should monitor what they read, checking that the word they have decoded fits in with what else they have read and makes sense in the context of what they already know about the topic.

The meaning of new words should be explained to pupils within the context of what they are reading, and they should be encouraged to use morphology, such as prefixes, to work out unknown words.

Pupils should learn about cause and effect in both narrative and non-fiction (for example, what has prompted a character's behaviour in a story; why certain dates are commemorated annually). 'Thinking aloud' when reading to pupils may help them to understand what skilled readers do.

Deliberate steps should be taken to increase pupils' vocabulary and their awareness of grammar so that they continue to understand the differences between spoken and written language.

Discussion should be demonstrated to pupils. They should be guided to participate in it and they should be helped to consider the opinions of others. They should receive feedback on their discussions.

Role play and other drama techniques can help pupils to identify with and explore characters. In these ways, they extend their understanding of what they read and have opportunities to try out the language they have listened to.

Year 2 Programme of Study (statutory requirements)	Notes and guidance (non-statutory)
• participate in discussion about books, poems and other works that are read to them and those that they can read for themselves, taking turns and listening to what others say • explain and discuss their understanding of books, poems and other material, both those that they listen to and those that they read for themselves.	

WRITING
Transcription
Spelling (see English Appendix 1)
Pupils should be taught to:
• spell by:
    • segmenting spoken words into phonemes and representing these by graphemes, spelling many correctly
    • learning new ways of spelling phonemes for which one or more spellings are already known, and learn some words with each spelling, including a few common homophones
    • learning to spell common exception words
    • learning to spell more words with contracted forms
    • learning the possessive apostrophe (singular), for example, the girl's book
    • distinguishing between homophones and near-homophones
• add suffixes to spell longer words, eg -*ment*, -*ness*, -*ful*, -*less*, -*ly*
• apply spelling rules and guidelines, as listed in English Appendix 1
• write from memory simple sentences dictated by the teacher that include words using the GPCs, common exception words and punctuation taught so far.
	WRITING
	Transcription
	Spelling
	In Year 2, pupils move towards more word-specific knowledge of spelling, including homophones. The process of spelling should be emphasised: that is, that spelling involves segmenting spoken words into phonemes and then representing all the phonemes by graphemes in the right order. Pupils should do this both for single-syllable and multi-syllabic words.
	
	At this stage children's spelling should be phonically plausible, even if not always correct. Misspellings of words that pupils have been taught should be corrected; other misspelt words can be used as an opportunity to teach pupils about alternative ways of representing those sounds.
	
	Pupils should be encouraged to apply their knowledge of suffixes from their word reading to their spelling. They should also draw from and apply their growing knowledge of word and spelling structure, as well as their knowledge of root words.

Year 2 Programme of Study (statutory requirements)

Handwriting

Pupils should be taught to:

- form lower-case letters of the correct size relative to one another
- start using some of the diagonal and horizontal strokes needed to join letters and understand which letters, when adjacent to one another, are best left unjoined
- write capital letters and digits of the correct size, orientation and relationship to one another and to lower-case letters
- use spacing between words that reflects the size of the letters.

Composition

Pupils should be taught to:

- develop positive attitudes towards and stamina for writing by:
  - writing narratives about personal experiences and those of others (real and fictional)
  - writing about real events
  - writing poetry
  - writing for different purposes
- consider what they are going to write before beginning by:
  - planning or saying out loud what they are going to write about
  - writing down ideas and/or key words, including new vocabulary
  - encapsulating what they want to say, sentence by sentence
- make simple additions, revisions and corrections to their own writing by:
  - evaluating their writing with the teacher and other pupils
  - re-reading to check that their writing makes sense and that verbs to indicate time are used correctly and consistently, including verbs in the continuous form
  - proofreading to check for errors in spelling, grammar and punctuation (for example, ends of sentences punctuated correctly)
- read aloud what they have written with appropriate intonation to make the meaning clear.

Notes and guidance (non-statutory)

Handwriting

Pupils should revise and practise correct letter formation frequently. They should be taught to write with a joined style as soon as they can form letters securely with the correct orientation.

Composition

Reading and listening to whole books, not simply extracts, helps pupils to increase their vocabulary and grammatical knowledge, including their knowledge of the vocabulary and grammar of Standard English. These activities also help them to understand how different types of writing, including narratives, are structured. All these can be drawn on for their writing.

Pupils should understand, through being shown, the skills and processes essential to writing: that is, thinking aloud as they collect ideas, drafting and re-reading to check their meaning is clear.

Drama and role play can contribute to the quality of pupils' writing by providing opportunities for pupils to develop and order their ideas by playing roles and improvising scenes in various settings.

Pupils might draw on and use new vocabulary from their reading, their discussions about it (one-to-one and as a whole class) and from their wider experiences.

Year 2 Programme of Study (statutory requirements)	Notes and guidance (non-statutory)
Vocabulary, grammar and punctuation	*Vocabulary, grammar and punctuation*
Pupils should be taught to:	The terms for discussing language should be embedded for pupils in the course of discussing their writing with them. Their attention should be drawn to the technical terms they need to learn.
• develop their understanding of the concepts set out in English Appendix 2 by:	
• learning how to use both familiar and new punctuation correctly (see English Appendix 2), including full stops, capital letters, exclamation marks, question marks, commas for lists and apostrophes for contracted forms and the possessive (singular)	
• learn how to use:	
• sentences with different forms: statement, question, exclamation, command	
• expanded noun phrases to describe and specify, *for example, the blue butterfly*	
• the present and past tenses correctly and consistently including the progressive form	
• subordination (using *when, if, that,* or *because*) and coordination (using *or, and,* or *but*)	
• the grammar for Year 2 in English Appendix 2	
• some features of written Standard English	
• use and understand the grammatical terminology in English Appendix 2 in discussing their writing.	

Lower Key Stage 2 – Years 3–4

By the beginning of Year 3, pupils should be able to read books written at an age-appropriate interest level. They should be able to read them accurately and at a speed that is sufficient for them to focus on understanding what they read rather than on decoding individual words. They should be able to decode most new words outside their spoken vocabulary, making a good approximation to the word's pronunciation. As their decoding skills become increasingly secure, teaching should be directed more towards developing their vocabulary and the breadth and depth of their reading, making sure that they become independent, fluent and enthusiastic readers who read widely and frequently. They should be developing their understanding and enjoyment of stories, poetry, plays and non-fiction, and learning to read silently. They should also be developing their knowledge and skills in reading non-fiction about a wide range of subjects. They should be learning to justify their views about what they have read: with support at the start of Year 3 and increasingly independently by the end of Year 4.

Pupils should be able to write down their ideas with a reasonable degree of accuracy and with good sentence punctuation. Teachers should therefore be consolidating pupils' writing skills, their vocabulary, their grasp of sentence structure and their knowledge of linguistic terminology. Teaching them to develop as writers involves teaching them to enhance the effectiveness of what they write as well as increasing their competence. Teachers should make sure that pupils build on what they have learned, particularly in terms of the range of their writing and the more varied grammar, vocabulary and narrative structures from which they can draw on to express their ideas. Pupils should be beginning to understand how writing can be different from speech. Joined handwriting should be the norm; pupils should be able to use it fast enough to keep pace with what they want to say. Pupils' spelling of common words should be correct, including exception words and other words that they have learned (see English Appendix 1). Pupils should spell words as accurately as possible using their phonic knowledge and other knowledge of spelling, such as morphology and etymology.

Most pupils will not need further direct teaching of word reading skills: they are able to decode unfamiliar words accurately, and need very few repeated experiences of this before the word is stored in such a way that they can read it without overt sound-blending. They should demonstrate understanding of figurative language, distinguish shades of meaning among related words and use age-appropriate, academic vocabulary. As in Key Stage 1, however, pupils who are still struggling to decode need to be taught to do this urgently through a rigorous and systematic phonics programme so that they catch up rapidly with their peers. If they cannot decode independently and fluently, they will find it increasingly difficult to understand what they read and to write down what they want to say. As far as possible, however, they should follow the Year 3 and 4 Programme of Study in terms of listening to new books, hearing and learning new vocabulary and grammatical structures, and discussing these.

Specific requirements for pupils to discuss what they are learning and to develop their wider skills in spoken language form part of this Programme of Study. In Years 3 and 4, pupils should become more familiar with and confident in using language in a greater variety of situations, for a variety of audiences and purposes, including through drama, formal presentations and debate.

Years 3–4 Programme of Study (statutory requirements)	Notes and guidance (non-statutory)
READING **Word reading** Pupils should be taught to: • apply their growing knowledge of root words, prefixes and suffixes (etymology and morphology) as listed in English Appendix 1, both to read aloud and to understand the meaning of new words they meet • read further exception words, noting the unusual correspondences between spelling and sound, and where these occur in the word.	**READING** **Word reading** At this stage, teaching comprehension should be taking precedence over teaching word reading directly. Any focus on word reading should support the development of vocabulary. When pupils are taught to read longer words, they should be supported to test out different pronunciations. They will attempt to match what they decode to words they may have already heard but may not have seen in print: for example, in reading *technical*, the pronunciation /tɛtʃnɪkəl/ ('technical') might not sound familiar, but /tɛknɪkəl/ ('teknical') should.

Years 3–4 Programme of Study (statutory requirements)	Notes and guidance (non-statutory)
READING	**READING**
Comprehension	**Comprehension**
Pupils should be taught to:	The focus should continue to be on pupils' comprehension as a primary element in reading. The knowledge and skills that pupils need in order to comprehend are very similar at different ages. This is why the Programmes of Study for comprehension in Years 3 and 4 and Years 5 and 6 are similar: the complexity of the writing increases the level of challenge.
• develop positive attitudes to reading and understanding of what they read by:	
• listening to and discussing a wide range of fiction, poetry, plays, non-fiction and reference books or textbooks	Pupils should be taught to recognise themes in what they read, such as the triumph of good over evil or the use of magical devices in fairy stories and folk tales.
• reading books that are structured in different ways and reading for a range of purposes	
• using dictionaries to check the meaning of words that they have read	They should also learn the conventions of different types of writing, (for example, the greeting in letters, a diary written in the first person or the use of presentational devices such as numbering and headings in instructions).
• increasing their familiarity with a wide range of books, including fairy stories, myths and legends, and retelling some of these orally	
• identifying themes and conventions in a wide range of books	Pupils should be taught to use the skills they have learned earlier and continue to apply these skills to read for different reasons, including for pleasure, or to find out information and the meaning of new words.
• preparing poems and play scripts to read aloud and to perform, showing understanding through intonation, tone, volume and action	
• discussing words and phrases that capture the reader's interest and imagination	Pupils should continue to have opportunities to listen frequently to stories, poems, non-fiction and other writing, including whole books and not just extracts, so that they build on what was taught previously. In this way, they also meet books and authors that they might not choose themselves. Pupils should also have opportunities to exercise choice in selecting books and be taught how to do so, with teachers making use of any available library services and expertise to support this.
• recognising some different forms of poetry (for example, free verse, narrative poetry)	
• understand what they read, in books they can read independently, by:	
• checking that the text makes sense to them, discussing their understanding and explaining the meaning of words in context	
• asking questions to improve their understanding of a text	
• drawing inferences such as inferring characters' feelings, thoughts and motives from their actions, and justifying inferences with evidence	
• predicting what might happen from details stated and implied	

Years 3–4 Programme of Study (statutory requirements)	Notes and guidance (non-statutory)
- identifying main ideas drawn from more than one paragraph and summarising these - identifying how language, structure, and presentation contribute to meaning - retrieve and record information from non-fiction - participate in discussion about both books that are read to them and those they can read for themselves, taking turns and listening to what others say.	Reading, re-reading and rehearsing poems and plays for presentation and performance give pupils opportunities to discuss language, including vocabulary, extending their interest in the meaning and origin of words. Pupils should be encouraged to use drama approaches to understand how to perform plays and poems to support their understanding of the meaning. These activities also provide them with an incentive to find out what expression is required, so feeding into comprehension. In using non-fiction, pupils should know what information they need to look for before they begin and be clear about the task. They should be shown how to use contents pages and indexes to locate information. Pupils should have guidance about the kinds of explanations and questions that are expected from them. They should help to develop, agree on, and evaluate rules for effective discussion. The expectation should be that all pupils take part.
WRITING **Transcription** *Spelling* (see English Appendix 1) Pupils should be taught to: - use further prefixes and suffixes and understand how to add them (English Appendix 1) - spell further homophones - spell words that are often misspelt (English Appendix 1) - place the possessive apostrophe accurately in words with regular plurals (for example, girls', boys') and in words with irregular plurals (for example, children's) - use the first two or three letters of a word to check its spelling in a dictionary - write from memory simple sentences, dictated by the teacher, that include words and punctuation taught so far.	**WRITING** **Transcription** *Spelling* Pupils should learn to spell new words correctly and have plenty of practice in spelling them. As in Years 1 and 2, pupils should continue to be supported in understanding and applying the concepts of word structure (see English Appendix 2). Pupils need sufficient knowledge of spelling in order to use dictionaries efficiently.

Years 3–4 Programme of Study (statutory requirements)	Notes and guidance (non-statutory)
Handwriting Pupils should be taught to: • use the diagonal and horizontal strokes that are needed to join letters and understand which letters, when adjacent to one another, are best left unjoined • increase the legibility, consistency and quality of their handwriting, for example by ensuring that the downstrokes of letters are parallel and equidistant; that lines of writing are spaced sufficiently so that the ascenders and descenders of letters do not touch.	*Handwriting* Pupils should be using joined handwriting throughout their independent writing. Handwriting should continue to be taught, with the aim of increasing the fluency with which pupils are able to write down what they want to say. This, in turn, will support their composition and spelling.

Composition
 	
Pupils should be taught to:
 	
• plan their writing by:
  • discussing writing similar to that which they are planning to write in order to understand and learn from its structure, vocabulary and grammar
  • discussing and recording ideas
• draft and write by:
  • composing and rehearsing sentences orally (including dialogue), progressively building a varied and rich vocabulary and an increasing range of sentence structures (English Appendix 2)
  • organising paragraphs around a theme
  • in narratives, creating settings, characters and plot
  • in non-narrative material, using simple organisational devices for example, headings and subheadings
• evaluate and edit by:
  • assessing the effectiveness of their own and others' writing and suggesting improvements
  • proposing changes to grammar and vocabulary to improve consistency, including the accurate use of pronouns in sentences
• proofread for spelling and punctuation errors
• read aloud their own writing, to a group or the whole class, using appropriate intonation and controlling the tone and volume so that the meaning is clear.
	Composition
	
	Pupils should continue to have opportunities to write for a range of real purposes and audiences as part of their work across the curriculum. These purposes and audiences should underpin the decisions about the form the writing should take, such as a narrative, an explanation or a description.
	
	Pupils should understand, through being shown these, the skills and processes that are essential for writing: that is, thinking aloud to explore and collect ideas, drafting, and re-reading to check their meaning is clear, including doing so as the writing develops. Pupils should be taught to monitor whether their own writing makes sense in the same way that they monitor their reading, checking at different levels.

Years 3–4 Programme of Study (statutory requirements)	Notes and guidance (non-statutory)

Vocabulary, grammar and punctuation
 	
Pupils should be taught to:
 	
• develop their understanding of the concepts set out in English Appendix 2 by:
 	
  • extending the range of sentences with more than one clause by using a wider range of conjunctions, including *when, if, because, although*
 	
  • using the present perfect form of verbs in contrast to the past tense
 	
  • choosing nouns or pronouns appropriately for clarity and cohesion and to avoid repetition
 	
  • using conjunctions, adverbs and prepositions to express time and cause
 	
  • using fronted adverbials
 	
• learning the grammar for Years 3 and 4 in English Appendix 2
 	
• indicate grammatical and other features by:
 	
  • using commas after fronted adverbials
 	
  • indicating possession by using the possessive apostrophe with plural nouns
 	
  • using and punctuating direct speech
 	
• use and understand the grammatical terminology in English Appendix 2 accurately and appropriately when discussing their writing and reading.
	Vocabulary, grammar and punctuation
	
	Grammar should be taught explicitly: pupils should be taught the terminology and concepts set out in English Appendix 2, and be able to apply them correctly to examples of real language, such as their own writing or books that they have read.
	
	At this stage, pupils should start to learn about some of the differences between Standard English and non-Standard English and begin to apply what they have learned, for example, in writing dialogue for characters.

Upper Key Stage 2 – Years 5–6

By the beginning of Year 5, pupils should be able to read aloud a wider range of poetry and books written at an age-appropriate interest level with accuracy and at a reasonable speaking pace. They should be able to read most words effortlessly and to work out how to pronounce unfamiliar written words with increasing automaticity. If the pronunciation sounds unfamiliar, they should ask for help in determining both the meaning of the word and how to pronounce it correctly.

They should be able to prepare readings, with appropriate intonation to show their understanding, and should be able to summarise and present a familiar story in their own words. They should be reading widely and frequently, outside as well as in school, for pleasure and information. They should be able to read silently, and then discuss what they have read.

Pupils should be able to write down their ideas quickly. Their grammar and punctuation should be broadly accurate. Pupils' spelling of most words taught so far should be accurate and they should be able to spell words that they have not yet been taught by using what they have learned about how spelling works in English.

During Years 5 and 6, teachers should continue to emphasise pupils' enjoyment and understanding of language, especially vocabulary, to support their reading and writing. Pupils' knowledge of language, gained from stories, plays, poetry, non-fiction and textbooks, will support their increasing fluency as readers, their facility as writers, and their comprehension. As in Years 3 and 4, pupils should be taught to enhance the effectiveness of their writing as well as their competence.

It is essential that pupils whose decoding skills are poor are taught through a rigorous and systematic phonics programme so that they catch up rapidly with their peers in terms of their decoding and spelling. However, as far as possible, these pupils should follow the upper Key Stage 2 Programme of Study in terms of listening to books and other writing that they have not come across before, hearing and learning new vocabulary and grammatical structures, and having a chance to talk about all of these.

By the end of Year 6, pupils' reading and writing should be sufficiently fluent and effortless for them to manage the general demands of the curriculum in Year 7, across all subjects and not just in English, but there will continue to be a need for pupils to learn subject-specific vocabulary. They should be able to reflect their understanding of the audience for and purpose of their writing by selecting appropriate vocabulary and grammar. Teachers should prepare pupils for secondary education by ensuring that they can consciously control the structure of sentences in their writing and understand why sentences are constructed as they are. This involves consolidation, practice and discussion of language.

Specific requirements for pupils to discuss what they are learning and to develop their wider skills in spoken language form part of this Programme of Study. In Years 5 and 6, pupils' confidence, enjoyment and mastery of language should be extended through public speaking, performance and debate.

Years 5–6 Programme of Study (statutory requirements)	Notes and guidance (non-statutory)
READING **Word reading** Pupils should be taught to: • apply their growing knowledge of root words, prefixes and suffixes (morphology and etymology), as listed in English Appendix 1, both to read aloud and to understand the meaning of new words that they meet.	**READING** **Word reading** At this stage, there should be no need for further direct teaching of word reading skills for almost all pupils. If pupils are struggling or failing in this, the reasons for this should be investigated. It is imperative that pupils are taught to read during their last two years at primary school if they enter Year 5 not being able to do so. Pupils should be encouraged to work out any unfamiliar word. They should focus on all the letters in a word so that they do not, for example, read 'invitation' for 'imitation' simply because they might be more familiar with the first word. Accurate reading of individual words, which might be key to the meaning of a sentence or paragraph, improves comprehension. When teachers are reading with or to pupils, attention should be paid to new vocabulary – both a word's meaning(s) and its correct pronunciation.

Years 5–6 Programme of Study (statutory requirements)	Notes and guidance (non-statutory)

READING
 	
Comprehension
 	
Pupils should be taught to:
 	
• maintain positive attitudes to reading and understanding of what they read by:
 	
  • continuing to read and discuss an increasingly wide range of fiction, poetry, plays, non-fiction and reference books or textbooks
 	
  • reading books that are structured in different ways and reading for a range of purposes
 	
  • increasing their familiarity with a wide range of books, including myths, legends and traditional stories, modern fiction, fiction from our literary heritage, and books from other cultures and traditions
 	
  • recommending books that they have read to their peers, giving reasons for their choices
 	
  • identifying and discussing themes and conventions in and across a wide range of writing
 	
  • making comparisons within and across books
 	
  • learning a wider range of poetry by heart
 	
  • preparing poems and plays to read aloud and to perform, showing understanding through intonation, tone and volume so that the meaning is clear to an audience
 	
• understand what they read by:
 	
  • checking that the book makes sense to them, discussing their understanding and exploring the meaning of words in context
 	
  • asking questions to improve their understanding
 	
  • drawing inferences such as inferring characters' feelings, thoughts and motives from their actions, and justifying inferences with evidence
 	
  • predicting what might happen from details stated and implied
 	
  • summarising the main ideas drawn from more than one paragraph, identifying key details that support the main ideas
	READING
	
	Comprehension
	
	Even though pupils can now read independently, reading aloud to them should include whole books so that they meet books and authors that they might not choose to read themselves.
	
	The knowledge and skills that pupils need in order to comprehend are very similar at different ages. Pupils should continue to apply what they have already learned to more complex writing.
	
	Pupils should be taught to recognise themes in what they read, such as loss or heroism. They should have opportunities to compare characters, consider different accounts of the same event and discuss viewpoints (both of authors and of fictional characters), within a text and across more than one text.
	
	They should continue to learn the conventions of different types of writing, such as the use of the first person in writing diaries and autobiographies.
	
	Pupils should be taught the technical and other terms needed for discussing what they hear and read, such as *metaphor, simile, analogy, imagery, style* and *effect*.
	
	In using reference books, pupils need to know what information they need to look for before they begin and need to understand the task. They should be shown how to use contents pages and indexes to locate information.
	
	The skills of information retrieval that are taught should be applied, for example, in reading history, geography and science textbooks, and in contexts where pupils are genuinely motivated to find out information, for example, reading information leaflets before a gallery or museum visit or reading a theatre programme or review. Teachers should consider making use of any available library services and expertise to support this.
	
	Pupils should have guidance about and feedback on the quality of their explanations and contributions to discussions.

Years 5–6 Programme of Study (statutory requirements)	Notes and guidance (non-statutory)
• identifying how language, structure and presentation contribute to meaning • discuss and evaluate how authors use language, including figurative language, considering the impact on the reader • distinguish between statements of fact and opinion • retrieve, record and present information from non-fiction • participate in discussions about books that are read to them and those they can read for themselves, building on their own and others' ideas and challenging views courteously • explain and discuss their understanding of what they have read, including through formal presentations and debates, maintaining a focus on the topic and using notes where necessary • provide reasoned justifications for their views.	Pupils should be shown how to compare characters, settings, themes and other aspects of what they read.
WRITING **Transcription** *Spelling* (see English Appendix 1) Pupils should be taught to: • use further prefixes and suffixes and understand the guidelines for adding them • spell some words with 'silent' letters, for example, *knight, psalm, solemn* • continue to distinguish between homophones and other words which are often confused • use knowledge of morphology and etymology in spelling and understand that the spelling of some words needs to be learned specifically, as listed in English Appendix 1 • use dictionaries to check the spelling and meaning of words • use the first three or four letters of a word to check spelling, meaning or both of these in a dictionary • use a thesaurus.	**WRITING** **Transcription** *Spelling* As in earlier years, pupils should continue to be taught to understand and apply the concepts of word structure so that they can draw on their knowledge of morphology and etymology to spell correctly.

Years 5–6 Programme of Study (statutory requirements)	Notes and guidance (non-statutory)
Handwriting and presentation Pupils should be taught to: • write legibly, fluently and with increasing speed by: • choosing which shape of a letter to use when given choices and deciding, as part of their personal style, whether or not to join specific letters • choosing the writing implement that is best suited for a task.	*Handwriting and presentation* Pupils should continue to practise handwriting and be encouraged to increase the speed of it, so that problems with forming letters do not get in the way of their writing down what they want to say. They should be clear about what standard of handwriting is appropriate for a particular task, for example, quick notes or a final handwritten version. They should also be taught to use an unjoined style, for example, for labelling a diagram or data, writing an email address, or for algebra and capital letters, for example, for filling in a form.
Composition Pupils should be taught to: • plan their writing by: • identifying the audience for and purpose of the writing, selecting the appropriate form and using other similar writing as models for their own • noting and developing initial ideas, drawing on reading and research where necessary • in writing narratives, considering how authors have developed characters and settings in what they have read, listened to or seen performed • draft and write by: • selecting appropriate grammar and vocabulary, understanding how such choices can change and enhance meaning • in narratives, describing settings, characters and atmosphere and integrating dialogue to convey character and advance the action • précising longer passages • using a wide range of devices to build cohesion within and across paragraphs • using further organisational and presentational devices to structure text and to guide the reader (for example, headings, bullet points, underlining)	**Composition** Pupils should understand, through being shown, the skills and processes essential for writing: that is, thinking aloud to generate ideas, drafting and re-reading to check that the meaning is clear.

Years 5–6 Programme of Study (statutory requirements)	Notes and guidance (non-statutory)

• evaluate and edit by:
  • assessing the effectiveness of their own and others' writing
  • proposing changes to vocabulary, grammar and punctuation to enhance effects and clarify meaning
  • ensuring the consistent and correct use of tense throughout a piece of writing
  • ensuring correct subject and verb agreement when using singular and plural, distinguishing between the language of speech and writing and choosing the appropriate register
• proofread for spelling and punctuation errors
• perform their own compositions, using appropriate intonation, volume and movement so that meaning is clear.	

Years 5–6 Programme of Study (statutory requirements)	Notes and guidance (non-statutory)

Vocabulary, grammar and punctuation
 	
Pupils should be taught to:
 	
• develop their understanding of the concepts set out in English Appendix 2 by:
 	
  • recognising vocabulary and structures that are appropriate for formal speech and writing, including subjunctive forms
 	
  • using passive verbs to affect the presentation of information in a sentence
 	
  • using the perfect form of verbs to mark relationships of time and cause
 	
  • using expanded noun phrases to convey complicated information concisely
 	
  • using modal verbs or adverbs to indicate degrees of possibility
 	
  • using relative clauses beginning with *who, which, where, when, whose, that* or with an implied (ie omitted) relative pronoun
 	
  • learning the grammar for Years 5–6 in English Appendix 2
 	
• indicate grammatical and other features by:
 	
  • using commas to clarify meaning or avoid ambiguity in writing
 	
  • using hyphens to avoid ambiguity
 	
  • using brackets, dashes or commas to indicate parenthesis
 	
  • using semi-colons, colons or dashes to mark boundaries between independent clauses
 	
  • using a colon to introduce a list
 	
  • punctuating bullet points consistently
 	
• use and understand the grammatical terminology in English Appendix 2 accurately and appropriately in discussing their writing and reading.
	Vocabulary, grammar and punctuation
	
	Pupils should continue to add to their knowledge of linguistic terms, including those to describe grammar, so that they can discuss their writing and reading.

English Appendix 1: Spelling

Most people read words more accurately than they spell them. The younger pupils are, the truer this is.

By the end of Year 1, pupils should be able to read a large number of different words containing the GPCs that they have learned, whether or not they have seen these words before. Spelling, however, is a very different matter. Once pupils have learned more than one way of spelling particular sounds, choosing the right letter or letters depends on their either having made a conscious effort to learn the words or having absorbed them less consciously through their reading. Younger pupils have not had enough time to learn or absorb the accurate spelling of all the words that they may want to write.

This appendix provides examples of words embodying each pattern which is taught. Many of the words listed as 'example words' for Years 1 and 2, including almost all those listed as 'exception words', are used frequently in pupils' writing, and therefore it is worth pupils learning the correct spelling. The 'exception words' contain GPCs which have not yet been taught as widely applicable, but this may be because they are applicable in very few age-appropriate words rather than because they are rare in English words in general.

The wordlists for Years 3 and 4 and Years 5 and 6 are statutory. The lists are a mixture both of words pupils frequently use in their writing and those which they often misspell. Some of the listed words may be thought of as quite challenging, but the 100 words in each list can be covered in fewer than two school years if teachers simply add words each week.

The rules and guidance are intended to support the teaching of spelling. Phonic knowledge should continue to underpin spelling after Key Stage 1; teachers should still draw pupils' attention to GPCs that do and do not fit in with what has been taught so far. Increasingly, however, pupils also need to understand the role of morphology and etymology. Although particular GPCs in root words simply have to be learned, teachers can help pupils to understand relationships between meaning and spelling where these are relevant. For example, understanding the relationship between *medical* and *medicine* may help pupils to spell the /s/ sound in *medicine* with the letter 'c'. Pupils can also be helped to spell words with prefixes and suffixes correctly if they understand some general principles for adding them. Teachers should be familiar with what pupils have been taught about spelling in earlier years, such as which rules pupils have been taught for adding prefixes and suffixes.

In this spelling appendix, the left-hand column is statutory; the middle and right-hand columns are non-statutory guidance.

The International Phonetic Alphabet (IPA) is used to represent sounds (phonemes). A table showing the IPA is provided in this document.

Year 1

Spelling – work for Year 1		
Statutory requirements		
Revision of Reception work The boundary between revision of work covered in Reception and the introduction of new work may vary according to the programme used, but basic revision should include: • all letters of the alphabet and the sounds which they most commonly represent • consonant digraphs which have been taught and the sounds which they represent • vowel digraphs which have been taught and the sounds which they represent • the process of segmenting spoken words into sounds before choosing graphemes to represent the sounds • words with adjacent consonants • guidance and rules which have been taught.		
Statutory requirements	**Rules and guidance (non-statutory)**	**Example words (non-statutory)**
The sounds /f/, /l/, /s/, /z/ and /k/ spelt ff, ll, ss, zz and ck	The /f/, /l/, /s/, /z/ and /k/ sounds are usually spelt as **ff, ll, ss, zz** and **ck** if they come straight after a single vowel letter in short words. **Exceptions:** *if, pal, us, bus, yes.*	off, well, miss, buzz, back
The /ŋ/ sound spelt n before k		bank, think, honk, sunk
Division of words into syllables	Each syllable is like a 'beat' in the spoken word. Words of more than one syllable often have an unstressed syllable in which the vowel sound is unclear.	pocket, rabbit, carrot, thunder, sunset
-tch	The /tʃ/ sound is usually spelt as **tch** if it comes straight after a single vowel letter. **Exceptions:** *rich, which, much, such.*	catch, fetch, kitchen, notch, hutch

Rule	Explanation	Examples
The /v/ sound at the end of words	English words hardly ever end with the letter **v**, so if a word ends with a /v/ sound, the letter **e** usually needs to be added after the 'v'.	have, live, give
Adding s and es to words (plural of nouns and the third person singular of verbs)	If the ending sounds like /s/ or /z/, it is spelt as -s. If the ending sounds like /ɪz/ and forms an extra syllable or 'beat' in the word, it is spelt as -**es**.	cats, dogs, spends, rocks, thanks, catches
Adding the endings -ing, -ed and -er to verbs where no change is needed to the root word	-**ing** and -**er** always add an extra syllable to the word and -**ed** sometimes does. The past tense of some verbs may sound as if it ends in /ɪd/ (extra syllable), /d/ or /t/ (no extra syllable), but all these endings are spelt -**ed**. If the verb ends in two consonant letters (the same or different), the ending is simply added on.	hunting, hunted, hunter, buzzing, buzzed, buzzer, jumping, jumped, jumper
Adding -er and -est to adjectives where no change is needed to the root word	As with verbs (see above), if the adjective ends in two consonant letters (the same or different), the ending is simply added on.	grander, grandest, fresher, freshest, quicker, quickest
Vowel digraphs and trigraphs	Some may already be known, depending on the programmes used in Reception, but some will be new.	
ai oi	The digraphs **ai** and **oi** are virtually never used at the end of English words.	rain, wait, train, paid, afraid oil, join, coin, point, soil
ay oy	**ay** and **oy** are used for those sounds at the end of words and at the end of syllables.	day, play, say, way, stay boy, toy, enjoy, annoy
a–e		made, came, same, take, safe
e–e		these, theme, complete
i–e		five, ride, like, time, side
o–e		home, those, woke, hope, hole
u–e	Both the /u:/ and /ju:/ ('oo' and 'yoo') sounds can be spelt as **u–e**.	June, rule, rude, use, tube, tune
ar		car, start, park, arm, garden
ee		see, tree, green, meet, week
ea (/iː/)		sea, dream, meat, each, read (present tense)
ea (/ɛ/)		head, bread, meant, instead, read (past tense)
er (/ɜː/)		(stressed sound): her, term, verb, person
er (/ə/)		(unstressed schwa sound): better, under, summer, winter, sister
ir		girl, bird, shirt, first, third
ur		turn, hurt, church, burst, Thursday

oo (/u:/)	Very few words end with the letters oo, although the few that do are often words that primary children in Year 1 will encounter, for example, zoo	food, pool, moon, zoo, soon
oo (/ʊ/)		book, took, foot, wood, good
oa	The digraph oa is rare at the end of an English word.	boat, coat, road, coach, goal
oe		toe, goes
ou	The only common English word ending in ou is you.	out, about, mouth, around, sound
ow (/aʊ/) ow (/əʊ/) ue ew	Both the /u:/ and /ju:/ ('oo' and 'yoo') sounds can be spelt as u–e, ue and ew. If words end in the /oo/ sound, ue and ew are more common spellings than oo.	now, how, brown, down, town own, blow, snow, grow, show blue, clue, true, rescue, Tuesday new, few, grew, flew, drew, threw
ie (/aɪ/)		lie, tie, pie, cried, tried, dried
ie (/i:/)		chief, field, thief
igh		high, night, light, bright, right
or		for, short, born, horse, morning
ore		more, score, before, wore, shore
aw		saw, draw, yawn, crawl
au		author, August, dinosaur, astronaut
air		air, fair, pair, hair, chair
ear		dear, hear, beard, near, year
ear (/ɛə/)		bear, pear, wear
are (/ɛə/)		bare, dare, care, share, scared
Words ending -y (/i:/ or /ɪ/)		very, happy, funny, party, family
New consonant spellings ph and wh	The /f/ sound is not usually spelt as ph in short everyday words (eg fat, fill, fun).	dolphin, alphabet, phonics, elephant when, where, which, wheel, while
Using k for the /k/ sound	The /k/ sound is spelt as k rather than as c before e, i and y.	Kent, sketch, kit, skin, frisky
Adding the prefix un-	The prefix un– is added to the beginning of a word without any change to the spelling of the root word.	unhappy, undo, unload, unfair, unlock
Compound words	Compound words are two words joined together. Each part of the longer word is spelt as it would be if it were on its own.	football, playground, farmyard, bedroom, blackberry
Common exception words	Pupils' attention should be drawn to the grapheme–phoneme correspondences that do and do not fit in with what has been taught so far.	the, a, do, to, today, of, said, says, are, were, was, is, his, has, I, you, your, they, be, he, me, she, we, no, go, so, by, my, here, there, where, love, come, some, one, once, ask, friend, school, put, push, pull, full, house, our – and/or others, according to the programme used.

Year 2

Spelling – revision of work from Year 1	As words with new GPCs are introduced, many previously-taught GPCs can be revised at the same time as these words will usually contain them.	
Spelling – new work for Year 2		
Statutory requirements	**Rules and guidance (non-statutory)**	**Example words (non-statutory)**
The /dʒ/ sound spelt as ge and dge at the end of words, and sometimes spelt as g elsewhere in words before e, i and y	The letter 'j' is never used for the /dʒ/ ('dge') sound at the end of English words. At the end of a word, the /dʒ/ sound is spelt -**dge** straight after the /æ/, /ɛ/, /ɪ/, /ɒ/, /ʌ/ and /ʊ/ sounds (sometimes called 'short' vowels). After all other sounds, whether vowels or consonants, the /dʒ/ sound is spelt as -**ge** at the end of a word. In other positions in words, the /dʒ/ sound is often (but not always) spelt as g before e, i, and y. The /dʒ/ sound is always spelt as j before a, o and u.	badge, edge, bridge, dodge, fudge age, huge, change, charge, bulge, village gem, giant, magic, giraffe, energy jacket, jar, jog, join, adjust
The /s/ sound spelt c before e, i and y		race, ice, cell, city, fancy
The /n/ sound spelt kn and (less often) gn at the beginning of words	The 'k' and 'g' at the beginning of these words was sounded hundreds of years ago.	knock, know, knee, gnat, gnaw
The /r/ sound spelt wr at the beginning of words	This spelling probably also reflects an old pronunciation.	write, written, wrote, wrong, wrap
The /l/ or /əl/ sound spelt -le at the end of words	The -**le** spelling is the most common spelling for this sound at the end of words.	table, apple, bottle, little, middle
The /l/ or /əl/ sound spelt -el at the end of words	The -**el** spelling is much less common than -**le**. The -**el** spelling is used after **m, n, r, s, v, w** and more often than not after **s**.	camel, tunnel, squirrel, travel, towel, tinsel
The /l/ or /əl/ sound spelt -al at the end of words	Not many nouns end in -**al**, but many adjectives do.	metal, pedal, capital, hospital, animal
Words ending -il	There are not many of these words.	pencil, fossil, nostril
The /aɪ/ sound spelt -y at the end of words	This is by far the most common spelling for this sound at the end of words.	cry, fly, dry, try, reply, July
Adding -es to nouns and verbs ending in -y	The **y** is changed to **i** before -**es** is added.	flies, tries, replies, copies, babies, carries
Adding -ed, -ing, -er and -est to a root word ending in -y with a consonant before it.	The **y** is changed to **i** before -**ed**, -**er** and -**est** are added, but not before -**ing** as this would result in **ii**. The only ordinary words with **ii** are *skiing* and *taxiing*.	copied, copier, happier, happiest, cried, replied ...**but** copying, crying, replying

Rule	Description	Examples
Adding the endings -ing, -ed, -er, -est and -y to words ending in -e with a consonant before it	The -e at the end of the root word is dropped before -ing, -ed, -er, -est, -y or any other suffix beginning with a vowel letter is added. The exception is *being*.	hiking, hiked, hiker, nicer, nicest, shiny
Adding -ing, -ed, -er, -est and -y to words of one syllable ending in a single consonant letter after a single vowel letter	The last consonant letter of the root word is doubled to keep the /æ/, /ɛ/, /ɪ/, /ɒ/ and /ʌ/ sound (ie to keep the vowel 'short'). **Exception:** The letter 'x' is never doubled: *mixing, mixed, boxer, sixes*.	patting, patted, humming, hummed, dropping, dropped, sadder, saddest, fatter, fattest, runner, runny
The /ɔː/ sound spelt a before l and ll	The /ɔː/ sound ('or') is usually spelt as **a** before **l** and **ll**.	all, ball, call, walk, talk, always
The /ʌ/ sound spelt o		other, mother, brother, nothing, Monday
The /iː/ sound spelt -ey	The plural of these words is formed by the addition of **-s** (*donkeys, monkeys,* etc).	key, donkey, monkey, chimney, valley
The /ɒ/ sound spelt a after w and qu	a is the most common spelling for the /ɒ/ ('h<u>o</u>t') sound after **w** and **qu**.	want, watch, wander, quantity, squash
The /ɜː/ sound spelt or after w	There are not many of these words.	word, work, worm, world, worth
The /ɔː/ sound spelt ar after w	There are not many of these words.	war, warm, towards
The /ʒ/ sound spelt s		television, treasure, usual
The suffixes -ment, -ness, -ful, -less and -ly	If a suffix starts with a consonant letter, it is added straight on to most root words without any change to the last letter of those words. **Exceptions:** (1) *argument* (2) root words ending in **-y** with a consonant before it but only if the root word has more than one syllable.	enjoyment, sadness, careful, playful, hopeless, plainness (plain + ness), badly, merriment, happiness, plentiful, penniless, happily
Contractions	In contractions, the apostrophe shows where a letter or letters would be if the words were written in full (eg *can't* – *cannot*). *It's* means *it is* (eg *It's raining*) or sometimes *it has* (eg *It's been raining*), but *its* is never used for the possessive.	can't, didn't, hasn't, couldn't, it's, I'll
The possessive apostrophe (singular nouns)		Megan's, Ravi's, the girl's, the child's, the man's
Words ending in -tion		station, fiction, motion, national, section
Homophones and near-homophones	It is important to know the difference in meaning between homophones.	there/their/they're, here/hear, quite/quiet, see/sea, bare/bear, one/won, sun/son, to/too/two, be/bee, blue/blew, night/knight

Common exception words	Some words are exceptions in some accents but not in others – eg *past, last, fast, path* and *bath* are not exceptions in accents where the **a** in these words is pronounced /æ/, as in *cat*. *Great, break* and *steak* are the only common words where the /eɪ/ sound is spelt **ea**.	door, floor, poor, because, find, kind, mind, behind, child, children*, wild, climb, most, only, both, old, cold, gold, hold, told, every, everybody, even, great, break, steak, pretty, beautiful, after, fast, last, past, father, class, grass, pass, plant, path, bath, hour, move, prove, improve, sure, sugar, eye, could, should, would, who, whole, any, many, clothes, busy, people, water, again, half, money, Mr, Mrs, parents, Christmas – and/or others according to programme used. * Note: 'children' is not an exception to what has been taught so far but is included because of its relationship with 'child'.

Years 3 and 4

	Rules and guidance (non-statutory)	Example words (non-statutory)
Spelling – revision of work from Years 1 and 2	Pay special attention to the rules for adding suffixes.	
Spelling – new work for Years 3 and 4		
Statutory requirements	**Rules and guidance (non-statutory)**	**Example words (non-statutory)**
Adding suffixes beginning with vowel letters to words of more than one syllable	If the last syllable of a word is stressed and ends with one consonant letter which has just one vowel letter before it, the final consonant letter is doubled before any ending beginning with a vowel letter is added. The consonant letter is not doubled if the syllable is unstressed.	forgetting, forgotten, beginning, beginner, prefer, preferred gardening, gardener, limiting, limited, limitation
The /ɪ/ sound spelt y elsewhere than at the end of words	These words should be learned as needed.	myth, gym, Egypt, pyramid, mystery
The /ʌ/ sound spelt ou	These words should be learned as needed.	young, touch, double, trouble, country
More prefixes	Most prefixes are added to the beginning of root words without any changes in spelling, but see **in-** below. Like **un-**, the prefixes **dis-** and **mis-** have negative meanings. The prefix **in-** can mean both 'not' and 'in'/'into'. In the words given here it means 'not'. Before a root word starting with **l**, **in-** becomes **il**. Before a root word starting with **m** or **p**, **in-** becomes **im-**. Before a root word starting with **r**, **in-** becomes **ir-**. **re-** means 'again' or 'back'. **sub-** means 'under'. **inter-** means 'between' or 'among'. **super-** means 'above'. **anti-** means 'against'. **auto-** means 'self' or 'own'.	**dis-**, **mis-**: disappoint, disagree, disobey misbehave, mislead, misspell (mis + spell) **in-**: inactive, incorrect illegal, illegible immature, immortal, impossible, impatient, imperfect irregular, irrelevant, irresponsible **re-**: redo, refresh, return, reappear, redecorate **sub-**: subdivide, subheading, submarine, submerge **inter-**: interact, intercity, international, interrelated (inter + related) **super-**: supermarket, superman, superstar **anti-**: antiseptic, anti-clockwise, antisocial **auto-**: autobiography, autograph
The suffix -ation	The suffix **-ation** is added to verbs to form nouns. The rules already learned still apply.	information, adoration, sensation, preparation, admiration
The suffix -ly	The suffix **-ly** is added to an adjective to form an adverb. The rules already learned still apply. The suffix **-ly** starts with a consonant letter, so it is added straight on to most root words.	sadly, completely, usually (usual + ly), finally (final + ly), comically (comical + ly)

Category	Rule / Notes	Examples
The suffix -ly	**Exceptions:** (1) If the root word ends in -y with a consonant letter before it, the y is changed to i, but only if the root word has more than one syllable. (2) If the root word ends with -le, the -le is changed to -ly. (3) If the root word ends with -ic, -ally is added rather than just -ly, except in the word *publicly*. (4) The words *truly, duly, wholly*.	happily, angrily; gently, simply, humbly, nobly basically, frantically, dramatically
Words with endings sounding like /ʒə/ or /tʃə/	The ending sounding like /ʒə/ is always spelt **-sure**. The ending sounding like /tʃə/ is often spelt **-ture**, but check that the word is not a root word ending in **(t)ch** with an **er** ending – eg *teacher, catcher, richer, stretcher*.	measure, treasure, pleasure, enclosure creature, furniture, picture, nature, adventure
Endings which sound like /ʒən/	If the ending sounds like /ʒən/, it is spelt as **-sion**	division, invasion, confusion, decision, collision, television
The suffix -ous	Sometimes the root word is obvious and the usual rules apply for adding suffixes beginning with vowel letters. Sometimes there is no obvious root word. **-our** is changed to **-or** before **-ous** is added. A final 'e' must be kept if the /dʒ/ sound of 'g' is to be kept. If there is an /iː/ sound before the **-ous** ending, it is usually spelt as **i**, but a few words have **e**.	poisonous, dangerous, mountainous, famous, various; tremendous, enormous, jealous; humorous, glamorous, vigorous; courageous, outrageous; serious, obvious, curious; hideous, spontaneous, courteous
Endings which sound like /ʃən/, spelt -tion, -sion, -ssion, -cian	Strictly speaking, the suffixes are **-ion** and **-cian**. Clues about whether to put **t, s, ss** or **c** before these suffixes often come from the last letter or letters of the root word. **-tion** is the most common spelling. It is used if the root word ends in **t** or **te**. **-ssion** is used if the root word ends in **ss** or **-mit**. **-sion** is used if the root word ends in **d** or **se**. **Exceptions:** *attend – attention, intend – intention*. **-cian** is used if the root word ends in **c** or **cs**.	invention, injection, action, hesitation, completion; expression, discussion, confession, permission, admission; expansion, extension, comprehension, tension; musician, electrician, magician, politician, mathematician
Words with the /k/ sound spelt ch (Greek in origin)		scheme, chorus, chemist, echo, character
Words with the /ʃ/ sound spelt ch (mostly French in origin)		chef, chalet, machine, brochure
Words ending with the /g/ sound spelt -gue and the /k/ sound spelt -que (French in origin)		league, tongue, antique, unique

Words with the /s/ sound spelt sc (Latin in origin)	In the Latin words from which these words come, the Romans probably pronounced the **c** and the **k** as two sounds rather than one – /s/ /k/	science, scene, discipline, fascinate, crescent
Words with the /eɪ/ sound spelt ei, eigh, or ey		vein, weigh, eight, neighbour, they, obey
Possessive apostrophe with plural words	The apostrophe is placed after the plural form of the word; **-s** is not added if the plural already ends in **-s**, but *is* added if the plural does not end in **-s** (ie is an irregular plural – eg *children's*).	girls', boys', babies', children's, men's, mice's (**Note**: singular proper nouns ending in an s use the 's suffix eg Cyprus's population)
Homophones or near-homophones		accept/except, affect/effect, ball/bawl, berry/bury, brake/break, fair/fare, grate/great, groan/grown, here/hear, heel/heal/he'll, knot/not, mail/male, main/mane, meat/meet, medal/meddle, missed/mist, peace/piece, plain/plane, rain/rein/reign, scene/seen, weather/whether, whose/who's

Word list for Years 3 and 4

accident(ally)	busy/business	describe	extreme	heart	library	ordinary	promise	strange
actual(ly)	calendar	different	famous	height	material	particular	purpose	strength
address	caught	difficult	favourite	history	medicine	peculiar	quarter	suppose
answer	centre	disappear	February	imagine	mention	perhaps	question	therefore
appear	century	early	forward(s)	important	minute	popular	regular	though/although
arrive	certain	earth	fruit	increase	natural	position	reign	thought
believe	circle	eight/eighth	grammar	interest	naughty	possess(ion)	remember	through
bicycle	complete	enough	group	island	notice	possible	sentence	various
breath	consider	exercise	guard	knowledge	occasion(ally)	potatoes	separate	weight
breathe	continue	experience	guide	learn	often	pressure	special	woman/women
build	decide	experiment	heard	length	opposite	probably	straight	

Teachers should continue to emphasise to pupils the relationships between sounds and letters, even when the relationships are unusual. Once root words are learned in this way, longer words can be spelled correctly, if the rules and guidelines for adding prefixes and suffixes are also known.

Examples:

business: once *busy* is learned, with due attention to the unusual spelling of the /i/ sound as 'u', *business* can then be spelled as **busy** + **ness**, with the **y** of **busy** changed to **i** according to the rule.

disappear: the root word **appear** contains sounds which can be spelled in more than one way so it needs to be learned, but the prefix **dis-** is then simply added to **appear**.

Understanding the relationships between words can also help with spelling.

Examples:

bicycle is *cycle* (from the Greek for *wheel*) with **bi-** (meaning *two*) before it.

medicine is related to *medical* so the /s/ sound is spelt as **c**.

opposite is related to *oppose*, so the schwa sound in *opposite* is spelt as **o**.

Years 5 and 6

Spelling – revise work done in previous years		
Spelling – new work for Years 5 and 6		
Statutory requirements	**Rules and guidance (non-statutory)**	**Example words (non-statutory)**
Endings which sound like /ʃəs/ spelt -cious or -tious	Not many common words end like this. If the root word ends in **-ce**, the /ʃ/ sound is usually spelt as **c** – eg *vice – vicious, grace – gracious, space – spacious, malice – malicious.* **Exception:** *anxious.*	vicious, precious, conscious, delicious, malicious, suspicious, ambitious, cautious, fictitious, infectious, nutritious
Endings which sound like /ʃəl/	**-cial** is common after a vowel letter and **-tial** after a consonant letter, but there are some exceptions. **Exceptions:** initial, financial, commercial, provincial (the spelling of the last three is clearly related to *finance, commerce* and *province*).	official, special, artificial, partial, confidential, essential
Words ending in -ant, -ance/-ancy, -ent, -ence/-ency	Use **-ant** and **-ance/-ancy** if there is a related word with a /æ/ or /eɪ/ sound in the right position; **-ation** endings are often a clue. Use **-ent** and **-ence/-ency** after soft **c** (/s/ sound), soft **g** (/dʒ/ sound) and **qu**, or if there is a related word with a clear /ʃ/ sound in the right position. There are many words, however, where the above guidelines don't help. These words just have to be learned.	observant, observance, (observation), expectant (expectation), hesitant, hesitancy (hesitation), tolerant, tolerance (toleration), substance (substantial) innocent, innocence, decent, decency, frequent, frequency, confident, confidence (confidential) assistant, assistance, obedient, obedience, independent, independence
Words ending in -able and -ible **Words ending in -ably and -ibly**	The **-able/-ably** endings are far more common than the **-ible/-ibly** endings. As with **-ant** and **-ance/-ancy**, the **-able** ending is used if there is a related word ending in **-ation**. If the **-able** ending is added to a word ending in **-ce** or **-ge**, the **e** after the **c** or **g** must be kept as those letters would otherwise have their 'hard' sounds (as in *cap* and *gap*) before the **a** of the **-able** ending. The **-able** ending is usually but not always used if a complete root word can be heard before it, even if there is no related word ending in **-ation**. The first five examples opposite are obvious: in *reliable*, the complete word *rely* is heard, but the **y** changes to **i** in accordance with the rule. The **-ible** ending is common if a complete root word can't be heard before it but it also sometimes occurs when a complete word *can* be heard (eg *sensible*).	adorable/adorably (adoration), applicable/applicably (application), considerable/considerably (consideration), tolerable/tolerably (toleration) changeable, noticeable, forcible, legible dependable, comfortable, understandable, reasonable, enjoyable, reliable possible/possibly, horrible/horribly, terrible/terribly, visible/visibly, incredible/incredibly, sensible/sensibly

Category	Explanation	Examples
Adding suffixes beginning with vowel letters to words ending in -fer	The **r** is doubled if the **-fer** is still stressed when the ending is added. The **r** is not doubled if the **-fer** is no longer stressed.	referring, referred, referral, preferring, preferred, transferring, transferred reference, referee, preference, transference
Use of the hyphen	Hyphens can be used to join a prefix to a root word, especially if the prefix ends in a vowel letter and the root word also begins with one.	co-ordinate, re-enter, co-operate, co-own
Words with the /iː/ sound spelt ei after c	The 'i before e except after **c**' rule applies to words where the sound spelt by **ei** is /iː/. **Exceptions:** *protein, caffeine, seize* (and *either* and *neither* if pronounced with an initial /iː/ sound).	deceive, conceive, receive, perceive, ceiling
Words containing the letter-string ough	**ough** is one of the trickiest spellings in English – it can be used to spell a number of different sounds.	ought, bought, thought, nought, brought, fought rough, tough, enough cough though, although, dough through thorough, borough plough, bough
Words with 'silent' letters (ie letters whose presence cannot be predicted from the pronunciation of the word)	Some letters which are no longer sounded used to be sounded hundreds of years ago: eg in *knight*, there was a /k/ sound before the /n/, and the **gh** used to represent the sound that 'ch' now represents in the Scottish word *loch*.	doubt, island, lamb, solemn, thistle, knight
Homophones and other words that are often confused	In these pairs of words, nouns end **-ce** and verbs end **-se**. Advice and advise provide a useful clue as the word *advise* (verb) is pronounced with a /z/ sound – which could not be spelt **c**. More examples: aisle: a gangway between seats (in a church, train, plane) isle: an island aloud: out loud allowed: permitted affect: usually a verb (eg *The weather may affect our plans*) effect: usually a noun (eg *It may have an effect on our plans*). If a verb, it means 'bring about' (eg *He will effect changes in the running of the business.*). altar: a table-like piece of furniture in a church alter: to change	advice/advise device/devise licence/license practice/practise prophecy/prophesy farther: further father: a male parent guessed: past tense of the verb *guess* guest: visitor heard: past tense of the verb *hear* herd: a group of animals led: past tense of the verb *lead* lead: present tense of that verb, or else the metal which is very heavy (*as heavy as lead*)

ascent: the act of ascending (going up)
assent: to agree/agreement (verb and noun)

bridal: to do with a bride at a wedding
bridle: reins etc for controlling a horse

cereal: made from grain (eg breakfast cereal)
serial: adjective from the noun *series* – a succession of things one after the other

compliment: to make nice remarks about someone (verb) or the remark that is made (noun)
complement: related to the word *complete* – to make something complete or more complete (eg *her scarf complemented her outfit*)

descent: the act of descending (going down)
dissent: to disagree/disagreement (verb and noun)

desert: as a noun – a barren place (stress on first syllable); as a verb – to abandon (stress on second syllable)
dessert: (stress on second syllable) a sweet course after the main course of a meal

draft: noun – a first attempt at writing something; verb – to make the first attempt; also, to draw in someone (eg *to draft in extra help*)
draught: a current of air

morning: before noon
mourning: grieving for someone who has died

past: noun or adjective referring to a previous time (eg *In the past*) or preposition or adverb showing place (eg *he walked past me*)
passed: past tense of the verb 'pass' (eg *I passed him in the road*)

precede: go in front of or before
proceed: go on

principal: adjective – most important (eg *principal ballerina*); noun – important person (eg *principal of a college*)
principle: basic truth or belief

profit: money that is made in selling things
prophet: someone who foretells the future

stationary: not moving
stationery: paper, envelopes etc

steal: take something that does not belong to you
steel: metal

wary: cautious
weary: tired

who's: contraction of *who is* or *who has*
whose: belonging to someone (eg *Whose jacket is that?*)

Word list for Years 5 and 6

accommodate
accompany
according
achieve
aggressive
amateur
ancient
apparent
appreciate
attached
available
average
awkward
bargain
bruise
category
cemetery
committee

communicate
community
competition
conscience*
conscious*
controversy
convenience
correspond
criticise (critic + ise)
curiosity
definite
desperate
determined
develop
dictionary
disastrous
embarrass

environment
equip (-ped, -ment)
especially
exaggerate
excellent
existence
explanation
familiar
foreign
forty
frequently
government
guarantee
harass
hindrance
identity
immediate(ly)

individual
interfere
interrupt
language
leisure
lightning
marvellous
mischievous
muscle
necessary
neighbour
nuisance
occupy
occur
opportunity
parliament
persuade
physical

prejudice
privilege
profession
programme
pronunciation
queue
recognise
recommend
relevant
restaurant
rhyme
rhythm
sacrifice
secretary
shoulder
signature
sincere(ly)
soldier

stomach
sufficient
suggest
symbol
system
temperature
thorough
twelfth
variety
vegetable
vehicle
yacht

Teachers should continue to emphasise to pupils the relationships between sounds and letters, even when the relationships are unusual. Once root words are learned in this way, longer words can be spelled correctly if the rules and guidelines for adding prefixes and suffixes are also known. Many of the words in the list above can be used for practice in adding suffixes.

Understanding the history of words and relationships between them can also help with spelling.

Examples:

* *Conscience* and *conscious* are related to *science*: *conscience* is simply *science* with the prefix *con-* added. These words come from the Latin word *scio* meaning *I know*.

The word *desperate*, meaning 'without hope', is often pronounced in English as *desp'rate*, but the *-sper-* part comes from the Latin *spero*, meaning 'I hope', in which the **e** was clearly sounded.

Familiar is related to *family*, so the /ə/ sound in the first syllable of *familiar* is spelt as **a**.

International Phonetic Alphabet

The table below shows each symbol of the International Phonetic Alphabet (IPA) and provides examples of the associated grapheme(s). [6]

The table is not a comprehensive alphabetic code chart; it is intended simply as guidance for teachers in understanding the IPA symbols used in the spelling appendix (English Appendix 1). The pronunciations in the table are, by convention, based on Received Pronunciation and could be significantly different from other accents.

Consonants

/b/	bad
/d/	dog
/ð/	this
/dʒ/	gem, jug
/f/	if, puff, photo
/g/	gum
/h/	how
/j/	yes
/k/	cat, check, key, school
/l/	leg, hill
/m/	man
/n/	man
/☒/	sing
/☒/	both
/p/	pet
/r/	red
/s/	sit, miss, cell
/ʃ/	she, chef
/t/	tea
/tʃ/	check
/v/	vet
/w/	wet, when
/z/	zip, hens, buzz
/ʒ/	pleasure

Vowels

/ɑː/	father, arm
/ɒ/	hot
/æ/	cat
/aɪ/	mind, fine, pie, high
/aʊ/	out, cow
/ɛ/	hen, head
/eɪ/	say, came, bait
/ɛə/	air
/əʊ/	cold, boat, cone, blow
/ɪ/	hit
/ɪə/	beer
/iː/	she, bead, see, scheme, chief
/ɔː/	launch, raw, born
/ɔɪ/	coin, boy
/ʊ/	book
/ʊə/	tour
/uː/	room, you, blue, brute
/ʌ/	cup
/ɜː/	fern, turn, girl
/ə/	farmer

---

[6] This chart is adapted slightly from the version provided on the DfE's website to support the Year 1 phonics screening check.

English Appendix 2: Vocabulary, grammar and punctuation

The grammar of our first language is learned naturally and implicitly through interactions with other speakers and from reading. Explicit knowledge of grammar is, however, very important, as it gives us more conscious control and choice in our language. Building this knowledge is best achieved through a focus on grammar within the teaching of reading, writing and speaking. Once pupils are familiar with a grammatical concept (for example 'modal verb'), they should be encouraged to apply and explore this concept in the grammar of their own speech and writing and to note where it is used by others. Young pupils, in particular, use more complex language in speech than in writing, and teachers should build on this, aiming for a smooth transition to sophisticated writing.

The table on page 74 focuses on Standard English and should be read in conjunction with the Programme of Study as it sets out the statutory requirements. The first column refers to the structure of words and vocabulary building. The table shows when concepts should be introduced first, not necessarily when they should be completely understood. It is very important, therefore, that the content in earlier years be revisited in subsequent years to consolidate knowledge and build on pupils' understanding. Teachers should also go beyond the content set out here if they feel it is appropriate.

The grammatical terms that pupils should learn are set out in the final column. They should learn to recognise and use the terminology through discussion and practice. All terms in bold should be understood with the meanings set out in the glossary.

Years 1 to 6 Detail of content to be introduced (statutory requirements)

Year	Word	Sentence	Text	Punctuation	Terminology for pupils
1	Regular **plural noun suffixes** -s or -es (for example, *dog, dogs; wish, wishes*), including the effects of these suffixes on the meaning of the noun. **Suffixes** that can be added to **verbs** where no change is needed in the spelling of root words (eg *helping, helped, helper*). How the **prefix** *un-* changes the meaning of **verbs** and **adjectives** (negation, *eg unkind*, or undoing, *eg untie the boat*).	How **words** can combine to make **sentences.** Joining **words** and joining **clauses** using *and.*	Sequencing **sentences** to form short narratives.	Separation of **words** with spaces. Introduction to capital letters, full stops, question marks and exclamation marks to demarcate **sentences.** Capital letters for names and for the personal **pronoun** *I*.	letter, capital letter word, singular, plural sentence punctuation, full stop, question mark, exclamation mark
2	Formation of **nouns** using **suffixes** such as *-ness*, *-er* and by compounding (eg *whiteboard, superman*). Formation of **adjectives** using **suffixes** such as *-ful*, *-less*. (A fuller list of **suffixes** can be found on page 63 in the Year 2 spelling section in English Appendix 1.) Use of the **suffixes** *-er*, *-est* in **adjectives** and *-ly* to turn adjectives into **adverbs.**	**Subordination** (using *when, if, that, because*) and coordination (using *or, and, but*). Expanded **noun phrases** for description and specification *(for example, the blue butterfly, plain flour, the man in the Moon).* How the grammatical patterns in a sentence indicate its function as a **statement, question, exclamation** or **command.**	Correct choice and consistent use of **present tense** and **past tense** throughout writing. Use of the **progressive** form of **verbs** in the **present** and **past tense** to mark actions in progress *(for example, she is drumming, he was shouting).*	Use of capital letters, full stops, question marks and exclamation marks to demarcate **sentences.** Commas to separate items in a list. **Apostrophes** to mark where letters are missing in spelling and to mark singular possession in nouns (for example, the girl's name).	noun, noun phrase statement, question, exclamation, command, compound, adjective, verb, suffix, adverb tense (past, present) apostrophe, comma

■ SCHOLASTIC

3	Formation of **nouns** using a range of **prefixes**, for example, *super-, anti-, auto-.* Use of the **forms** *a* or *an* according to whether the next **word** begins with a **consonant** or a **vowel** (for example, _a rock, an open box_). **Word families** based on common **words**, showing how words are related in form and meaning (for example, *solve, solution, solver, dissolve, insoluble*).	Expressing time, place and cause using **conjunctions** (for example, *when, before, after, while, so, because*), **adverbs** (for example, *then, next, soon, therefore*), or **prepositions** (for example, *before, after, during, in, because of*).	Introduction to paragraphs as a way to group related material. Headings and subheadings to aid presentation. Use of the **present perfect** form of **verbs** instead of the simple past (for example, *He has gone out to play* contrasted with *He went out to play*).	Introduction to inverted commas to **punctuate** direct speech.	adverb, preposition conjunction word family, prefix clause, subordinate clause direct speech consonant, consonant letter, vowel, vowel letter inverted commas (or 'speech marks')
4	The grammatical difference between **plural** and **possessive** -s. Standard English forms for **verb inflections** instead of local spoken forms (for example, *we were* instead of *we was*, or *I did* instead of *I done*).	Noun phrases expanded by the addition of modifying adjectives, nouns and preposition phrases (eg *the teacher* expanded to: *the strict maths teacher with curly hair*). **Fronted adverbials** (for example, _Later that day_, I heard the bad news.).	Use of paragraphs to organise ideas around a theme. Appropriate choice of **pronoun** or **noun** within and across **sentences** to aid cohesion and avoid repetition.	Use of inverted commas and other **punctuation** to indicate direct speech, for example, a comma after the reporting clause; end punctuation within inverted commas: *The conductor shouted, 'Sit down!'*). **Apostrophes** to mark singular and **plural** possession (for example, *the girl's name, the girls' names*) Use of commas after **fronted adverbials.**	determiner pronoun, possessive pronoun, adverbial

5	Converting **nouns** or **adjectives** into **verbs** using **suffixes** (for example, *-ate; -ise; -ify*). **Verb prefixes** (for example, *dis-, de-, mis-, over- and re-*).	**Relative clauses** beginning *with who, which, where, when, whose, that,* or an omitted relative pronoun. Indicating degrees of possibility using **adverbs** (for example, *perhaps, surely*) or **modal verbs** (for example, *might, should, will, must*).	Devices to build **cohesion** within a paragraph (for example, *then, after that, this, firstly*). Linking ideas across paragraphs using **adverbials** of time (for example, *later*), place (for example, *nearby*) and number (for example, *secondly*) or tense choices (for example, *he had seen her before*)	Brackets, dashes or commas to indicate parenthesis. Use of commas to clarify meaning or avoid ambiguity.	modal verb, relative pronoun relative clause parenthesis, bracket, dash cohesion, ambiguity
6	The difference between vocabulary typical of informal speech and vocabulary appropriate for formal speech and writing (for example, *find out – discover; ask for – request; go in – enter*). How words are related by meaning as synonyms and antonyms (eg *big, large, little*).	Use of the **passive** to affect the presentation of information in a **sentence** (for example, *I broke the window in the greenhouse* versus *The window in the greenhouse was broken [by me]*). The difference between structures typical of informal speech and structures appropriate for formal speech and writing (for example, the use of question tags: *He's your friend, isn't he?*, or the use of **subjunctive** forms such as *If I were* or *Were they to come* in some very formal writing and speech).	Linking ideas across paragraphs using a wider range of **cohesive devices**: repetition of a **word** or phrase, grammatical connections (for example, the use of adverbials such as *on the other hand, in contrast, or as a consequence*), and **ellipsis**. Layout devices, for example, headings, subheadings, columns, bullets, or tables, to structure text.	Use of the semi-colon, colon and dash to mark the boundary between independent **clauses** (for example, *It's raining; I'm fed up*). Use of the colon to introduce a list and use of semi-colons within lists. **Punctuation** of bullet points to list information. How hyphens can be used to avoid ambiguity (for example, *man eating shark* versus *man-eating shark*, or *recover* versus *re-cover*).	subject, object active, passive synonym, antonym ellipsis, hyphen, colon, semi-colon, bullet points

English Programme of Study: KS3

Purpose of study

English has a pre-eminent place in education and in society. A high-quality education in English will teach pupils to speak and write fluently so that they can communicate their ideas and emotions to others and, through their reading and listening, others can communicate with them. Through reading in particular, pupils have a chance to develop culturally, emotionally, intellectually, socially and spiritually. Literature, especially, plays a key role in such development. Reading also enables pupils both to acquire knowledge and to build on what they already know. All the skills of language are essential to participating fully as a member of society; pupils, therefore, who do not learn to speak, read and write fluently and confidently are effectively disenfranchised.

Aims

The overarching aim for English in the National Curriculum is to promote high standards of language and literacy by equipping pupils with a strong command of the spoken and written word, and to develop their love of literature through widespread reading for enjoyment. The National Curriculum for English aims to ensure that all pupils:

- read easily, fluently and with good understanding
- develop the habit of reading widely and often, for both pleasure and information
- acquire a wide vocabulary, an understanding of grammar and knowledge of linguistic conventions for reading, writing and spoken language
- appreciate our rich and varied literary heritage
- write clearly, accurately and coherently, adapting their language and style in and for a range of contexts, purposes and audiences
- use discussion in order to learn; they should be able to elaborate and explain clearly their understanding and ideas
- are competent in the arts of speaking and listening, making formal presentations, demonstrating to others and participating in debate.

Spoken language

The National Curriculum for English reflects the importance of spoken language in pupils' development across the whole curriculum – cognitively, socially and linguistically. Spoken language continues to underpin the development of pupils' reading and writing during Key Stage 3 and teachers should therefore ensure pupils' confidence and competence in this area continue to develop. Pupils should be taught to understand and use the conventions for discussion and debate, as well as continuing to develop their skills in working collaboratively with their peers to discuss reading, writing and speech across the curriculum.

Reading and writing

Reading at Key Stage 3 should be wide, varied and challenging. Pupils should be expected to read whole books, to read in depth and to read for pleasure and information.

Pupils should continue to develop their knowledge of and skills in writing, refining their drafting skills and developing resilience to write at length. They should be taught to write formal and academic essays as well as writing imaginatively. They should be taught to write for a variety of purposes and audiences across a range of contexts. This requires an increasingly wide knowledge of vocabulary and grammar.

Opportunities for teachers to enhance pupils' vocabulary will arise naturally from their reading and writing. Teachers should show pupils how to understand the relationships between words, how to understand nuances in meaning, and how to develop their understanding of, and ability to use, figurative language.

Pupils should be taught to control their speaking and writing consciously, understand why sentences are constructed as they are and to use Standard English. They should understand and use age-appropriate vocabulary, including linguistic and literary terminology, for discussing their reading, writing and spoken language. This involves consolidation, practice and discussion of language. It is important that pupils learn the correct grammatical terms in English and that these terms are integrated within teaching.

Teachers should build on the knowledge and skills that pupils have been taught at Key Stage 2. Decisions about progression should be based on the security of pupils' linguistic knowledge, skills and understanding, and their readiness to progress to the next stage. Pupils whose linguistic development is more advanced should be challenged through being offered opportunities for increased breadth and depth in reading and writing. Those who are less fluent should consolidate their knowledge, understanding and skills, including through additional practice.

Glossary

A non-statutory glossary is provided for teachers.

Attainment targets

By the end of Key Stage 3, pupils are expected to know, apply and understand the matters, skills and processes specified in the relevant Programme of Study.

Subject content

Reading

Pupils should be taught to:

- develop an appreciation and love of reading, and read increasingly challenging material independently through:
  - reading a wide range of fiction and non-fiction, including in particular whole books, short stories, poems and plays with a wide coverage of genres, historical periods, forms and authors. The range will include high-quality works from:
    - English literature, both pre-1914 and contemporary, including prose, poetry and drama
    - Shakespeare (two plays)
    - seminal world literature
  - choosing and reading books independently for challenge, interest and enjoyment.
  - re-reading books encountered earlier to increase familiarity with them and provide a basis for making comparisons.
- understand increasingly challenging texts through:
  - learning new vocabulary, relating it explicitly to known vocabulary and understanding it with the help of context and dictionaries
  - making inferences and referring to evidence in the text
  - knowing the purpose, audience for and context of the writing and drawing on this knowledge to support comprehension
  - checking their understanding to make sure that what they have read makes sense.
- read critically through:
  - knowing how language, including figurative language, vocabulary choice, grammar, text structure and organisational features, presents meaning
  - recognising a range of poetic conventions and understanding how these have been used
  - studying setting, plot and characterisation, and the effects of these
  - understanding how the work of dramatists is communicated effectively through performance and how alternative staging allows for different interpretations of a play
  - making critical comparisons across texts
  - studying a range of authors, including at least two authors in depth each year.

Writing

Pupils should be taught to:

- write accurately, fluently, effectively and at length for pleasure and information through:
  - writing for a wide range of purposes and audiences, including:
  - well-structured formal expository and narrative essays
  - stories, scripts, poetry and other imaginative writing
  - notes and polished scripts for talks and presentations
  - a range of other narrative and non-narrative texts, including arguments, and personal and formal letters
  - summarising and organising material, and supporting ideas and arguments with any necessary factual detail
  - applying their growing knowledge of vocabulary, grammar and text structure to their writing and selecting the appropriate form
  - drawing on knowledge of literary and rhetorical devices from their reading and listening to enhance the impact of their writing
- plan, draft, edit and proofread through:
  - considering how their writing reflects the audiences and purposes for which it was intended
  - amending the vocabulary, grammar and structure of their writing to improve its coherence and overall effectiveness
  - paying attention to accurate grammar, punctuation and spelling; applying the spelling patterns and rules set out in English Appendix 1 to the Key Stage 1 and 2 Programmes of Study for English.

Grammar and vocabulary

Pupils should be taught to:

- consolidate and build on their knowledge of grammar and vocabulary through:
  - extending and applying the grammatical knowledge set out in English Appendix 2 to the Key Stage 1 and 2 Programmes of Study to analyse more challenging texts
  - studying the effectiveness and impact of the grammatical features of the texts they read
  - drawing on new vocabulary and grammatical constructions from their reading and listening, and using these consciously in their writing and speech to achieve particular effects
  - knowing and understanding the differences between spoken and written language, including differences associated with formal and informal registers, and between Standard English and other varieties of English
  - using Standard English confidently in their own writing and speech
  - discussing reading, writing and spoken language with precise and confident use of linguistic and literary terminology.[7]

---

[7] Teachers should refer to the Glossary that accompanies the Programmes of Study for English for their own information on the range of terms used within the Programmes of Study as a whole.

Spoken English

Pupils should be taught to:

- speak confidently and effectively, including through:
  - using Standard English confidently in a range of formal and informal contexts, including classroom discussion
  - giving short speeches and presentations, expressing their own ideas and keeping to the point
  - participating in formal debates and structured discussions, summarising and/or building on what has been said
  - improvising, rehearsing and performing play scripts and poetry in order to generate language and discuss language use and meaning, using role, intonation, tone, volume, mood, silence, stillness and action to add impact.

Glossary for the Programmes of Study for English (non-statutory)

The following glossary includes all the technical grammatical terms used in the Programmes of Study for English, as well as others that might be useful. It is intended as an aid for teachers, not as the body of knowledge that should be learned by pupils. Apart from a few which are used only in schools (eg *root word*), the terms below are used with the meanings defined here in most modern books on English grammar. It is recognised that there are different schools of thought on grammar, but the terms defined here clarify those being used in the Programmes of Study. For further details, teachers should consult the many books that are available.

Terms in definitions

As in any tightly structured area of knowledge, grammar, vocabulary and spelling involve a network of technical concepts that help to define each other. Consequently, the definition of one concept builds on other concepts that are equally technical. Concepts that are defined elsewhere in the glossary are hyperlinked. For some concepts, the technical definition may be slightly different from the meaning that some teachers may have learned at school or may have been using with their own pupils; in these cases, the more familiar meaning is also discussed.

■SCHOLASTIC

Term	Definition	Examples
active voice	An active verb has its usual pattern of subject and object (in contrast with the passive).	Active: *The school arranged a visit.* Passive: *A visit was arranged by the school.*
adjective	The surest way to identify adjectives is by the ways they can be used: • before a noun, to make the noun's meaning more specific (ie to modify the noun), or • after the verb *be*, as its complement. Adjectives cannot be modified by other adjectives. This distinguishes them from nouns, which can be. Adjectives are sometimes called 'describing words' because they pick out single characteristics such as size or colour. This is often true, but it doesn't help to distinguish adjectives from other word classes, because verbs, nouns and adverbs can do the same thing.	*The pupils did some really good work.* [adjective used before a noun, to modify it] *Their work was good.* [adjective used after the verb *be*, as its complement] Not adjectives: *The lamp glowed.* [verb] *It was such a bright red!* [noun] *He spoke loudly.* [adverb] *It was a French grammar book.* [noun]
adverb	The surest way to identify adverbs is by the ways they can be used: they can modify a verb, an adjective, another adverb or even a whole clause. Adverbs are sometimes said to describe manner or time. This is often true, but it doesn't help to distinguish adverbs from other word classes that can be used as adverbials, such as preposition phrases, noun phrases and subordinate clauses.	*Usha soon started snoring loudly.* [adverbs modifying the verbs *started* and *snoring*] *That match was really exciting!* [adverb modifying the adjective *exciting*] *We don't get to play games very often.* [adverb modifying the other adverb, *often*] *Fortunately, it didn't rain.* [adverb modifying the whole clause 'it didn't rain' by commenting on it] Not adverbs: *Usha went up the stairs.* [preposition phrase used as adverbial] *She finished her work this evening.* [noun phrase used as adverbial] *She finished when the teacher got cross.* [subordinate clause used as adverbial]
adverbial	An adverbial is a word or phrase that is used, like an adverb, to modify a verb or clause. Of course, adverbs can be used as adverbials, but many other types of words and phrases can be used this way, including preposition phrases and subordinate clauses.	*The bus leaves in five minutes.* [preposition phrase as adverbial: modifies *leaves*] *She promised to see him last night.* [noun phrase modifying either *promised* or *see*, according to the intended meaning] *She worked until she had finished.* [subordinate clause as adverbial]
antonym	Two words are antonyms if their meanings are opposites.	*hot – cold* *light – dark* *light – heavy*
apostrophe	Apostrophes have two completely different uses: • showing the place of missing letters (eg *I'm* for *I am*) • marking possessives (eg *Hannah's mother*).	*I'm going out and I won't be long.* [showing missing letters] *Hannah's mother went to town in Justin's car.* [marking possessives]
article	The articles *the* (definite) and *a* or *an* (indefinite) are the most common type of determiner.	*The dog found a bone in an old box.*

Term	Definition	Examples
auxiliary verb	The auxiliary verbs are *be*, *have* and *do* and the modal verbs. They can be used to make questions and negative statements. In addition: • *be* is used in the progressive and passive • *have* is used in the perfect • *do* is used to form questions and negative statements if no other auxiliary verb is present	*They are winning the match.* [*be* used in the progressive] *Have you finished your picture?* [*have* used to make a question, and the perfect] *No, I don't know him.* [*do* used to make a negative; no other auxiliary is present] *Will you come with me or not?* [modal verb *will* used to make a question about the other person's willingness]
clause	A clause is a special type of phrase whose head is a verb. Clauses can sometimes be complete sentences. Clauses may be main or subordinate. Traditionally, a clause had to have a finite verb, but most modern grammarians also recognise non-finite clauses.	*It was raining.* [single-clause sentence] *It was raining but we were indoors.* [two finite clauses] *If you are coming to the party, please let us know.* [finite subordinate clause inside a finite main clause] *Usha went upstairs to play on her computer.* [non-finite clause]
cohesion	A text has cohesion if it is clear how the meanings of its parts fit together. Cohesive devices can help to do this. In the example, there are repeated references to the same thing (shown by the **bold text** and underlines), and the logical relations, such as time and cause, between different parts are clear.	*A visit* has been arranged for Year 6, to the ***Mountain Peaks Field Study Centre**, leaving school at 9.30am. **This** is **an overnight visit**. **The centre** has beautiful grounds and a **nature trail**. During the afternoon, the children will follow **the trail**.*
cohesive device	Cohesive devices are words used to show how the different parts of a text fit together. In other words, they create cohesion. Some examples of cohesive devices are: • determiners and pronouns, which can refer back to earlier words • conjunctions and adverbs, which can make relations between words clear • ellipsis of expected words.	*Julia's dad bought her a football. The football was expensive!* [determiner; refers us back to a particular football] *Joe was given a bike for Christmas. He liked it very much.* [the pronouns refer back to Joe and the bike] *We'll be going shopping before we go to the park.* [conjunction; makes a relationship of time clear] *I'm afraid we're going to have to wait for the next train. Meanwhile, we could have a cup of tea.* [adverb; refers back to time of waiting] *Where are you going? [...] To school!* [ellipsis of the expected words *I'm going*; links the answer back to the question]
complement	A verb's subject complement adds more information about its subject, and its object complement does the same for its object. Unlike the verb's object, its complement may be an adjective. The verb *be* normally has a complement.	*She is our teacher.* [adds more information about the subject, *she*] *They seem very competent.* [adds more information about the subject, *they*] *Learning makes me happy.* [adds more information about the object, *me*]
compound, compounding	A compound word contains at least two root words in its morphology; eg *whiteboard, superman*. Compounding is very important in English.	*blackbird, blow-dry, bookshop, ice-cream, English teacher, inkjet, one-eyed, bone-dry, baby-sit, daydream, outgrow*

Term	Definition	Examples
conjunction	A conjunction links two words or phrases together. There are two main types of conjunctions: • co-ordinating conjunctions (eg and) link two words or phrases together as an equal pair • subordinating conjunctions (eg when) introduce a subordinate clause.	James bought a bat *and* ball. [links the words *bat* and *ball* as an equal pair] Kylie is young *but* she can kick the ball hard. [links two clauses as an equal pair] Everyone watches *when Kyle does back-flips*. [introduces a subordinate clause] Joe can't practise kicking *because he's injured*. [introduces a subordinate clause]
consonant	A sound which is produced when the speaker closes off or obstructs the flow of air through the vocal tract, usually using lips, tongue or teeth. Most of the letters of the alphabet represent consonants. Only the letters a, e, i, o, u and y can represent vowel sounds.	/p/ [flow of air stopped by the lips, then released] /t/ [flow of air stopped by the tongue touching the roof of the mouth, then released] /f/ [flow of air obstructed by the bottom lip touching the top teeth] /s/ [flow of air obstructed by the tip of the tongue touching the gum line]
continuous	See progressive	
co-ordinate, co-ordination	Words or phrases are coordinated if they are linked as an equal pair by a coordinating conjunction (ie and, but, or). In the examples on the right, the co-ordinated elements are shown in the same colour, and the conjunction is underlined. The difference between coordination and subordination is that, in subordination, the two linked elements are not equal.	**Susan** *and* **Amra** met in a café. [links the words *Susan* and *Amra* as an equal pair] **They talked** *and* **drank tea** for an hour. [links two clauses as an equal pair] **Susan got a bus** *but* **Amra walked**. [links two clauses as an equal pair] Not coordination: They ate *before they met*. [*before* introduces a subordinate clause]
determiner	A determiner specifies a noun as known or unknown, and it goes before any modifiers (eg adjectives or other nouns). Some examples of determiners are: • articles (the, a or an) • demonstratives (eg this, those) • possessives (eg my, your) • quantifiers (eg some, every).	*the* home team [article, specifies the team as known] *a* good team [article, specifies the team as unknown] *that* pupil [demonstrative, known] *Julia's* parents [possessive, known] *some* big boys [quantifier, unknown] Contrast: home *the* team, big *some* boys [both incorrect, because the determiner should come before other modifiers]
digraph	A type of grapheme where two letters represent one phoneme. Sometimes, these two letters are not next to one another; this is called a split digraph.	The digraph *ea* in *each* is pronounced /iː/. The digraph *sh* in *shed* is pronounced /ʃ/. The split digraph *i–e* in *line* is pronounced /aɪ/.
ellipsis	Ellipsis is the omission of a word or phrase which is expected and predictable.	Frankie waved to Ivana and *she* watched her drive away. She did it because she wanted to *do it*.

Term	Definition	Example(s)
etymology	A word's etymology is its history: its origins in earlier forms of English or other languages, and how its form and meaning have changed. Many words in English have come from Greek, Latin or French.	The word *school* was borrowed from a Greek word ό÷ïëþ (*skholé*) meaning 'leisure'. The word *verb* comes from Latin *verbum*, meaning 'word'. The word *mutton* comes from French *mouton*, meaning 'sheep'.
finite verb	Every sentence typically has at least one verb which is either past or present tense. Such verbs are called 'finite'. The imperative verb in a command is also finite. Verbs that are not finite, such as participles or infinitives, cannot stand on their own: they are linked to another verb in the sentence.	*Lizzie does the dishes every day.* [present tense] *Even Hana did the dishes yesterday.* [past tense] *Do the dishes, Naser!* [imperative] Not finite verbs: • *I have done them.* [combined with the finite verb *have*] • *I will do them.* [combined with the finite verb *will*] • *I want to do them!* [combined with the finite verb *want*]
fronting, fronted	A word or phrase that normally comes after the <u>verb</u> may be moved before the verb: when this happens, we say it has been 'fronted'. For example, a fronted adverbial is an <u>adverbial</u> which has been moved before the verb. When writing fronted phrases, we often follow them with a comma.	*Before we begin, make sure you've got a pencil.* [Without fronting: *Make sure you've got a pencil before we begin.*] *The day after tomorrow, I'm visiting my granddad.* [Without fronting: *I'm visiting my granddad the day after tomorrow.*]
future	Reference to future time can be marked in a number of different ways in English. All these ways involve the use of a <u>present-tense verb</u>. See also <u>tense</u>. Unlike many other languages (such as French, Spanish or Italian), English has no distinct 'future tense' form of the verb comparable with its <u>present</u> and <u>past</u> tenses.	*He will leave tomorrow.* [present-tense *will* followed by infinitive *leave*] *He may leave tomorrow.* [present-tense *may* followed by infinitive *leave*] *He leaves tomorrow.* [present-tense *leaves*] *He is going to leave tomorrow.* [present tense *is* followed by *going to* plus the infinitive *leave*]
GPC	See <u>grapheme–phoneme correspondences</u>.	
grapheme	A letter, or combination of letters, that corresponds to a single <u>phoneme</u> within a word.	The grapheme *t* in the words *ten*, *bet* and *ate* corresponds to the phoneme /t/. The grapheme *ph* in the word *dolphin* corresponds to the phoneme /f/.
grapheme–phoneme correspondences	The links between letters, or combinations of letters, (graphemes) and the speech sounds (<u>phonemes</u>) that they represent. In the English writing system, graphemes may correspond to different phonemes in different words.	The grapheme s corresponds to the phoneme /s/ in the word *see*, but... ...it corresponds to the phoneme /z/ in the word *easy*.
head	See <u>phrase</u>	

Term	Definition	Examples
homonym	Two different words are homonyms if they both look exactly the same when written, and sound exactly the same when pronounced.	Has he _left_ yet? Yes – he went through the door on the _left_. The noise a dog makes is called a _bark_. Trees have _bark_.
homophone	Two different words are homophones if they sound exactly the same when pronounced.	_hear, here_ _some, sum_
infinitive	A verb's infinitive is the basic form used as the head-word in a dictionary (eg _walk, be_). Infinitives are often used: • after _to_ • after _modal verbs_.	I want to _walk_. I will _be_ quiet.
inflection	When we add _-ed_ to _walk_, or change _mouse_ to _mice_, this change of _morphology_ produces an inflection ('bending') of the basic word which has special grammar (eg _past tense_ or _plural_). In contrast, adding _-er_ to _walk_ produces a completely different word, _walker_, which is part of the same _word family_. Inflection is sometimes thought of as merely a change of ending, but, in fact, some words change completely when inflected.	_dogs_ is an inflection of _dog_. _went_ is an inflection of _go_. _better_ is an inflection of _good_.
intransitive verb	A verb which does not need an object in a sentence to complete its meaning. See 'transitive verb'.	We all _laughed_. We would like to _stay_ longer, but we must _leave_.
main clause	A _sentence_ contains at least one _clause_ which is not a _subordinate clause_; such a clause is a main clause. A main clause may contain any number of subordinate clauses.	_It was raining_ but _the sun was shining_. [Two main clauses] _The man who wrote it told me that it was true_. [One main clause containing two subordinate clauses.] _She said, 'It rained all day.'_ [One main clause containing another.]
modal verb	Modal verbs are used to change the meaning of other _verbs_. They can express meanings such as certainty, ability, or obligation. The main modal verbs are _will, would, can, could, may, might, shall, should, must_ and _ought_. A modal verb only has _finite_ forms and has no _suffixes_ (eg _I sing – he sings_, but not _I must – he musts_).	I _can_ do this maths work by myself. This ride _may_ be too scary for you! You _should_ help your little brother. Is it going to rain? Yes, it _might_. _Canning_ swim is important. [not possible because _can_ must be finite; contrast: _Being_ able to swim is important, where _being_ is not a modal verb]
modify, modifier	One word or phrase modifies another by making its meaning more specific. Because the two words make a _phrase_, the 'modifier' is normally close to the modified word.	In the phrase _primary-school teacher_: • _teacher_ is modified by _primary-school_ (to mean a specific kind of teacher) • _school_ is modified by _primary_ (to mean a specific kind of school).

Term	Definition	Examples
morphology	A word's morphology is its internal make-up in terms of root words and suffixes or prefixes, as well as other kinds of change such as the change of *mouse* to *mice*. Morphology may be used to produce different inflections of the same word (eg *boy – boys*), or entirely new words (eg *boy – boyish*) belonging to the same word family. A word that contains two or more root words is a compound (eg *news+paper, ice+cream*).	*dogs* has the morphological make-up: *dog* + *s*. *unhelpfulness* has the morphological make-up: *unhelpful* + *ness* • where *unhelpful* = *un* + *helpful* • and *helpful* = *help* + *ful*
noun	The surest way to identify nouns is by the ways they can be used after determiners such as *the*: for example, most nouns will fit into the frame 'The … matters/matter.' Nouns are sometimes called 'naming words' because they name people, places and 'things'; this is often true, but it doesn't help to distinguish nouns from other word classes. For example, prepositions can name places and verbs can name 'things' such as actions. Nouns may be classified as **common** (eg *boy, day*) or proper (eg *Ivan, Wednesday*), and also as **countable** (eg *thing, boy*) or non-countable (eg *stuff, money*). These classes can be recognised by the determiners they combine with.	*Our dog bit the burglar on his behind!* *My big brother did an amazing jump on his skateboard.* *Actions speak louder than words.* Not nouns: • *He's behind you!* [this names a place, but is a preposition, not a noun] • *She can jump so high!* [this names an action, but is a verb, not a noun] common, countable: *a book, books, two chocolates, one day, fewer ideas* common, non-countable: *money, some chocolate, less imagination* proper, countable: *Marilyn, London, Wednesday*
noun phrase	A noun phrase is a phrase with a noun as its head, eg *some foxes, foxes with bushy tails*. Some grammarians recognise one-word phrases, so that *foxes are multiplying* would contain the noun *foxes* acting as the head of the noun phrase *foxes*.	*Adult foxes can jump.* [*adult* modifies *foxes*, so *adult* belongs to the noun phrase] *Almost all healthy adult foxes in this area can jump.* [all the other words help to modify *foxes*, so they all belong to the noun phrase]
object	An object is normally a noun, pronoun or noun phrase that comes straight after the verb, and shows what the verb is acting upon. Objects can be turned into the subject of a passive verb, and cannot be adjectives (contrast with complements).	*Year 2 designed puppets.* [noun acting as object] *I like that.* [pronoun acting as object] *Some people suggested a pretty display.* [noun phrase acting as object] Contrast: • *A display was suggested.* [object of active verb becomes the subject of the passive verb] • *Year 2 designed pretty.* [incorrect, because adjectives cannot be objects]

participle	Verbs in English have two participles, called 'present participle' (eg *walking, taking*) and 'past participle' (eg *walked, taken*). Unfortunately, these terms can be confusing to learners, because: • they don't necessarily have anything to do with present or past time • although past participles are used as perfects (eg *has eaten*) they are also used as passives (eg *was eaten*).	*He is walking to school.* [present participle in a progressive] *He has taken the bus to school.* [past participle in a perfect] *The photo was taken in the rain.* [past participle in a passive]
passive	The sentence *It was eaten by our dog* is the passive of *Our dog ate it.* A passive is recognisable from: • the past participle form *eaten* • the normal object (*it*) turned into the subject • the normal subject (*our dog*) turned into an optional preposition phrase with *by* as its head • the verb *be* (*was*), or some other verb such as *get*. Contrast active. A verb is not 'passive' just because it has a passive meaning: it must be the passive version of an active verb.	*A visit was arranged by the school.* *Our cat got run over by a bus.* Active versions: • *The school arranged a visit.* • *A bus ran over our cat.* Not passive: • *He received a warning.* [past tense, active *received*] • *We had an accident.* [past tense, active *had*]
past tense	Verbs in the past tense are commonly used to: • talk about the past • talk about imagined situations • make a request sound more polite. Most verbs take a suffix *-ed*, to form their past tense, but many commonly-used verbs are irregular. See also tense.	*Tom and Chris showed me their new TV.* [names an event in the past] *Antonio went on holiday to Brazil.* [names an event in the past; irregular past of *go*] *I wish I had a puppy.* [names an imagined situation, not a situation in the past] *I was hoping you'd help tomorrow.* [makes an implied request sound more polite]
perfect	The perfect form of a verb generally calls attention to the consequences of a prior event; for example, *He has gone to lunch* implies that he is still away, in contrast with *He went to lunch.* It is formed by: • turning the verb into its past participle inflection • adding a form of the verb *have* before it. It can also be combined with the progressive (eg *he has been going*).	*She has downloaded some songs.* [present perfect; now she has some songs] *I had eaten lunch when you came.* [past perfect; I wasn't hungry when you came]

Term	Definition	Example
phoneme	A phoneme is the smallest unit of sound that signals a distinct, contrasting meaning. For example: • /t/ contrasts with /k/ to signal the difference between *tap* and *cap* • /t/ contrasts with /l/ to signal the difference between *bought* and *ball*. It is this contrast in meaning that tells us there are two distinct phonemes at work. There are around 44 phonemes in English; the exact number depends on regional accents. A single phoneme may be represented in writing by one, two, three or four letters constituting a single grapheme.	The word *cat* has three letters and three phonemes: /kæt/ The word *catch* has five letters and three phonemes: /katʃ/ The word *caught* has six letters and three phonemes: /kɔːt/
phrase	A phrase is a group of words that are grammatically connected so that they stay together, and that expand a single word, called the 'head'. The phrase is a noun phrase if its head is a noun, a preposition phrase if its head is a preposition, and so on; but if the head is a verb, the phrase is called a clause. Phrases can be made up of other phrases.	*She waved to her mother.* [A noun phrase, with the noun *mother* as its head] *She waved to her mother.* [A preposition phrase, with the preposition *to* as its head] *She waved to her mother.* [A clause, with the verb *waved* as its head]
plural	A plural noun normally has a suffix -s or -es and means 'more than one'. There are a few nouns with different morphology in the plural (eg *mice, formulae*).	*dogs* [more than one dog]; *boxes* [more than one box] *mice* [more than one mouse]
possessive	A possessive can be: • a noun followed by an apostrophe, with or without s • a possessive pronoun. The relation expressed by a possessive goes well beyond ordinary ideas of 'possession'. A possessive may act as a determiner.	*Tariq's book* [Tariq has the book] *The boys' arrival* [the boys arrive] *His obituary* [the obituary is about him] *That essay is mine.* [I wrote the essay]
prefix	A prefix is added at the beginning of a word in order to turn it into another word. Contrast suffix.	*overtake, disappear*
preposition	A preposition links a following noun, pronoun or noun phrase to some other word in the sentence. Prepositions often describe locations or directions, but can describe other things, such as relations of time. Words like *before* or *since* can act either as prepositions or as conjunctions.	*Tom waved goodbye to Christy. She'll be back from Australia in two weeks.* *I haven't seen my dog since this morning.* Contrast: *I'm going, since no-one wants me here!* [conjunction: links two clauses]

Term	Definition	Examples
preposition phrase	A preposition phrase has a preposition as its head followed by a noun, pronoun or noun phrase.	*He was in bed.* *I met them after the party.*
present tense	Verbs in the present tense are commonly used to: • talk about the present • talk about the future. They may take a suffix -s (depending on the subject). See also tense.	*Jamal goes to the pool every day.* [describes a habit that exists now] *He can swim.* [describes a state that is true now] *The bus arrives at three.* [scheduled now] *My friends are coming to play.* [describes a plan in progress now]
progressive	The progressive (also known as the 'continuous') form of a verb generally describes events in progress. It is formed by combining the verb's present participle (eg *singing*) with a form of the verb *be* (eg *he was singing*). The progressive can also be combined with the perfect (eg *he has been singing*).	*Michael is singing in the store room.* [present progressive] *Amanda was making a patchwork quilt.* [past progressive] *Usha had been practising for an hour when I called.* [past perfect progressive]
pronoun	Pronouns are normally used like nouns, except that: • they are grammatically more specialised • it is harder to modify them. In the examples, each sentence is written twice: once with nouns, and once with pronouns (underlined). Where the same thing is being talked about, the words are shown in bold.	**Amanda** *waved to* **Michael**. **She** *waved to* **him**. **John's** *mother is over there.* **His** *mother is over there.* *The* **visit** *will be an overnight* **visit**. **This** *will be an overnight* **visit**. **Simon** *broke it.* **He** *is the one* **who** *broke it.*
punctuation	Punctuation includes any conventional features of writing other than spelling and general layout: the standard punctuation marks . , ; : ? ! – – ( ) " " ' ' , and also word-spaces, capital letters, apostrophes, paragraph breaks and bullet points. One important role of punctuation is to indicate sentence boundaries.	*"I'm going out, Usha, and I won't be long," Mum said.*
Received Pronunciation	Received Pronunciation (often abbreviated to RP) is an accent which is used only by a small minority of English speakers in England. It is not associated with any one region. Because of its regional neutrality, it is the accent which is generally shown in dictionaries in the UK (but not, of course, in the USA). RP has no special status in the National Curriculum.	
register	Classroom lessons, football commentaries and novels use different registers of the same language, recognised by differences of vocabulary and grammar. Registers are 'varieties' of a language which are each tied to a range of uses, in contrast with dialects, which are tied to groups of users.	*I regret to inform you that Mr Joseph Smith has passed away.* [formal letter] *Have you heard that Joe has died?* [casual speech] *Joe falls down and dies, centre stage.* [stage direction]

Term	Definition	Examples
relative clause	A relative clause is a special type of <u>subordinate clause</u> that modifies a <u>noun</u>. It often does this by using a relative <u>pronoun</u> such as *who* or *that* to refer back to that noun, though the relative pronoun *that* is often omitted. A relative clause may also be attached to a <u>clause</u>. In that case, the pronoun refers back to the whole clause, rather than referring back to a noun. In the examples, the relative clauses are underlined, and the colour-coding pairs the pronouns with the words they refer back to.	That's the **boy who** lives near school. [*who* refers back to *boy*] The **prize that** I won was a book. [*that* refers back to *prize*] The **prize** I won was a book. [the pronoun *that* is omitted] **Tom broke the game, which** annoyed Ali. [*which* refers back to the whole clause]
root word	<u>Morphology</u> breaks words down into root words, which can stand alone, and <u>suffixes</u> or <u>prefixes</u>, which can't. For example, *help* is the root word for other words in its <u>word family</u> such as *helpful* and *helpless*, and also for its <u>inflections</u> such as *helping*. <u>Compound words</u> (eg *help-desk*) contain two or more root words. When looking in a dictionary, we sometimes have to look for the root word (or words) of the word we are interested in.	*played* [the root word is *play*] *unfair* [the root word is *fair*] *football* [the root words are *foot* and *ball*]
schwa	The name of a vowel sound that is found only in unstressed positions in English. It is the most common vowel sound in English. It is written as /ə/ in the International Phonetic Alphabet. In the English writing system, it can be written in many different ways.	/əlɒŋ/ [*along*] /bʌtə/ [*butter*] /dɒktə/ [*doctor*]
sentence	A sentence is a group of <u>words</u> which are grammatically connected to each other but not to any words outside the sentence. The form of a sentence's main clause shows whether it is being used as a statement, a question, a command or an exclamation. A sentence may consist of a single clause or it may contain several clauses held together by subordination or coordination. Classifying sentences as 'simple', 'complex' or 'compound' can be confusing, because a 'simple' sentence may be complicated, and a 'complex' one may be straightforward. The terms '**single-clause sentence**' and '**multi-clause sentence**' may be more helpful.	*John went to his friend's house.* *He stayed there till tea-time.* *John went to his friend's house, he stayed there till tea-time.* [This is a 'comma splice', a common error in which a comma is used where either a full stop or a semi-colon is needed to indicate the lack of any grammatical connection between the two clauses]. *You are my friend.* [statement] *Are you my friend?* [question] *Be my friend!* ['command'] *What a good friend you are!* [exclamation] *Ali went home on his bike to his goldfish and his current library book about pets.* [single-clause sentence] *She went shopping but took back everything she had bought because she didn't like any of it.* [multi-clause sentence]

Term	Definition	Example
split digraph	See digraph.	
Standard English	Standard English can be recognised by the use of a very small range of forms such as *those books*, *I did it* and *I wasn't doing anything* (rather than their non-Standard equivalents); it is not limited to any particular accent. It is the variety of English which is used, with only minor variation, as a major world language. Some people use Standard English all the time, in all situations from the most casual to the most formal, so it covers most <u>registers</u>. The aim of the National Curriculum is that everyone should be able to use Standard English as needed in writing and in relatively formal speaking.	*I did it because they were not willing to undertake any more work on those houses.* [formal Standard English] *I did it cos they wouldn't do any more work on those houses.* [casual Standard English] *I done it cos they wouldn't do no more work on them houses.* [casual non-Standard English]
stress	A <u>syllable</u> is stressed if it is pronounced more forcefully than the syllables next to it. The other syllables are unstressed.	a<u>bout</u> <u>vis</u>it
subject	The subject of a verb is normally the <u>noun</u>, <u>noun phrase</u> or <u>pronoun</u> that names the 'do-er' or 'be-er'. The subject's normal position is: • just before the <u>verb</u> in a statement • just after the <u>auxiliary verb</u>, in a question. Unlike the verb's <u>object</u> and <u>complement</u>, the subject can determine the form of the verb (eg *I am, you are*).	*Rula's mother went out.* *That is uncertain.* *The children will study the animals.* *Will the children study the animals?*
subjunctive	In some languages, the <u>inflections</u> of a <u>verb</u> include a large range of special forms which are used typically in <u>subordinate clauses</u>, and are called 'subjunctives'. English has very few such forms and those it has tend to be used in rather formal styles.	*The school requires that all pupils <u>be</u> honest.* *The school rules demand that pupils not <u>enter</u> the gym at lunchtime.* *If Zoë <u>were</u> the class president, things would be much better.*
subordinate, subordination	A subordinate word or phrase tells us more about the meaning of the word it is subordinate to. Subordination can be thought of as an unequal relationship between a subordinate word and a main word. For example: • an adjective is subordinate to the noun it <u>modifies</u> • <u>subjects</u> and <u>objects</u> are subordinate to their <u>verbs</u>. Subordination is much more common than the equal relationship of <u>coordination</u>. See also <u>subordinate clause</u>.	big dogs [*big* is subordinate to *dogs*] <u>Big dogs</u> need <u>long walks</u>. [*big dogs* and *long walks* are subordinate to *need*] *We can watch TV when we've finished.* [*when we've finished* is subordinate to *watch*]

Term	Definition	Examples
subordinate clause	A clause which is subordinate to some other part of the same sentence is a subordinate clause; for example, in *The apple that I ate was sour*, the clause *that I ate* is subordinate to *apple* (which it modifies). Subordinate clauses contrast with coordinate clauses as in *It was sour but looked very tasty*. (Contrast: main clause) However, clauses that are directly quoted as direct speech are not subordinate clauses.	*That's the street where Ben lives.* [relative clause; modifies *street*] *He watched her as she disappeared.* [adverbial; modifies *watched*] *What you said was very nice.* [acts as subject of *was*] *She noticed an hour had passed.* [acts as object of *noticed*] Not subordinate: *He shouted, 'Look out!'*
suffix	A suffix is an 'ending', used at the end of one word to turn it into another word. Unlike root words, suffixes cannot stand on their own as a complete word. Contrast prefix.	*call – called* *teach – teacher* [turns a verb into a noun] *terror – terrorise* [turns a noun into a verb] *green – greenish* [leaves word class unchanged]
syllable	A syllable sounds like a beat in a word. Syllables consist of at least one vowel, and possibly one or more consonants.	*Cat* has one syllable. *Fairy* has two syllables. *Hippopotamus* has five syllables.
synonym	Two words are synonyms if they have the same meaning, or similar meanings. Contrast antonym.	*talk – speak* *old – elderly*
tense	In English, tense is the choice between present and past verbs, which is special because it is signalled by inflections and normally indicates differences of time. In contrast, languages like French, Spanish and Italian have three or more distinct tense forms, including a future tense. (See also: future.) The simple tenses (present and past) may be combined in English with the perfect and progressive.	*He studies.* [present tense – present time] *He studied yesterday.* [past tense – past time] *He studies tomorrow, or else!* [present tense – future time] *He may study tomorrow.* [present tense + infinitive – future time] *He plans to study tomorrow.* [present tense + infinitive – future time] *If he studied tomorrow, he'd see the difference!* [past tense – imagined future] Contrast three distinct tense forms in Spanish: • *Estudia.* [present tense] • *Estudió.* [past tense] • *Estudiará.* [future tense]
transitive verb	A transitive verb takes at least one object in a sentence to complete its meaning, in contrast to an intransitive verb, which does not.	*He loves Juliet.* *She understands English grammar.*
trigraph	A type of grapheme where three letters represent one phoneme.	*High, pure, patch, hedge*
unstressed	See stressed.	

Term	Definition	Examples
verb	The surest way to identify verbs is by the ways they can be used: they can usually have a <u>tense</u>, either <u>present</u> or <u>past</u> (see also <u>future</u>). Verbs are sometimes called 'doing words' because many verbs name an action that someone does; while this can be a way of recognising verbs, it doesn't distinguish verbs from <u>nouns</u> (which can also name actions). Moreover many verbs name states or feelings rather than actions. Verbs can be classified in various ways: for example, as auxiliary, or <u>modal</u>; as <u>transitive</u> or <u>intransitive</u>; and as states or events.	*He <u>lives</u> in Birmingham.* [present tense] *The teacher <u>wrote</u> a song for the class.* [past tense] *He <u>likes</u> chocolate.* [present tense; not an action] *He <u>knew</u> my father.* [past tense; not an action] Not verbs: *The <u>walk</u> to Halina's house will take an hour.* [noun] *All that <u>surfing</u> makes Morwenna so sleepy!* [noun]
vowel	A vowel is a speech sound which is produced without any closure or obstruction of the vocal tract. Vowels can form <u>syllables</u> by themselves, or they may combine with <u>consonants</u>. In the English writing system, the letters *a, e, i, o, u* and *y* can represent vowels.	
word	A word is a unit of grammar: it can be selected and moved around relatively independently, but cannot easily be split. In punctuation, words are normally separated by word spaces. Sometimes, a sequence that appears grammatically to be two words is collapsed into a single written word, indicated with a hyphen or apostrophe (eg *well-built, he's*).	<u>headteacher</u> or <u>head teacher</u> [can be written with or without a space] *I'm* going out. <u>9.30am</u>
word class	Every <u>word</u> belongs to a word class which summarises the ways in which it can be used in grammar. The major word classes for English are: <u>noun</u>, <u>verb</u>, <u>adjective</u>, <u>adverb</u>, <u>preposition</u>, <u>determiner</u>, <u>pronoun</u>, <u>conjunction</u>. Word classes are sometimes called 'parts of speech'.	
word family	The <u>words</u> in a word family are normally related to each other by a combination of <u>morphology</u>, grammar and meaning.	<u>teach – teacher</u> <u>extend – extent – extensive</u> <u>grammar – grammatical – grammarian</u>

Babcock **ldp**
partners in education

Primary English & Mathematics

The Babcock LDP Primary English Adviser team work with schools and other organisations through:

- Sharing resources and ideas via a popular website **www.babcock-education.co.uk/ldp/literacy**. The site offers a wealth of free resources and support as well as signposts to publications which are practical ideas for the classroom.
- High quality training in all aspects of Primary English. Training can be centrally arranged or bespoke for individual schools or clusters of schools.
- Working alongside school improvement colleagues to support schools pre and post Ofsted including audit and action planning support.

Key areas supported by the team include:
- Planning for the New National Curriculum
- Grammar, Spelling and Phonics
- Talk for Writing
- Developing the teaching of reading: guided reading, Reciprocal Reading, reading for pleasure and researched reading interventions.

To find out more about the work of the team, visit our website and sign up for our newsletter, or contact: **rebecca.cosgrave@babcockinternational.com** **www.babcock-education.co.uk/ldp/literacy**

The Babcock LDP Primary Maths Adviser team work with schools and their partners to support the development of mathematics across the primary years.

All our work is underpinned by research and is based on the belief that thinking is at the heart of mathematics and therefore at the heart of mathematics teaching and learning.

The maths team holds the National Centre for Excellence in Teaching of Mathematics – National CPD Standard and are NCETM Professional Development Accredited Leads.

To find out more about the work of the team, visit our website and sign up for our newsletter, or contact: **ruth.trundley@babcockinternational.com** **www.babcock-education.co.uk/ldp/maths**

" This project has had a fantastic impact upon all learners who have received the intervention. "
(Assistant headteacher, West Croft)

" Thank you again for today – I know that the staff will have really appreciated seeing an actual guided group being taught 'live' and admired your bravery as well as the skills that you demonstrated. "
(Primary School headteacher, Bickleigh Down)

Working in partnership for better outcomes